Anton L. Becker

First Steps in German Idioms

Containing an alphabetical list of idioms, explanatory notes and examination

papers

Anton L. Becker

First Steps in German Idioms
Containing an alphabetical list of idioms, explanatory notes and examination papers

ISBN/EAN: 9783337085353

Printed in Europe, USA, Canada, Australia, Japan

Cover: Foto ©Paul-Georg Meister /pixelio.de

More available books at **www.hansebooks.com**

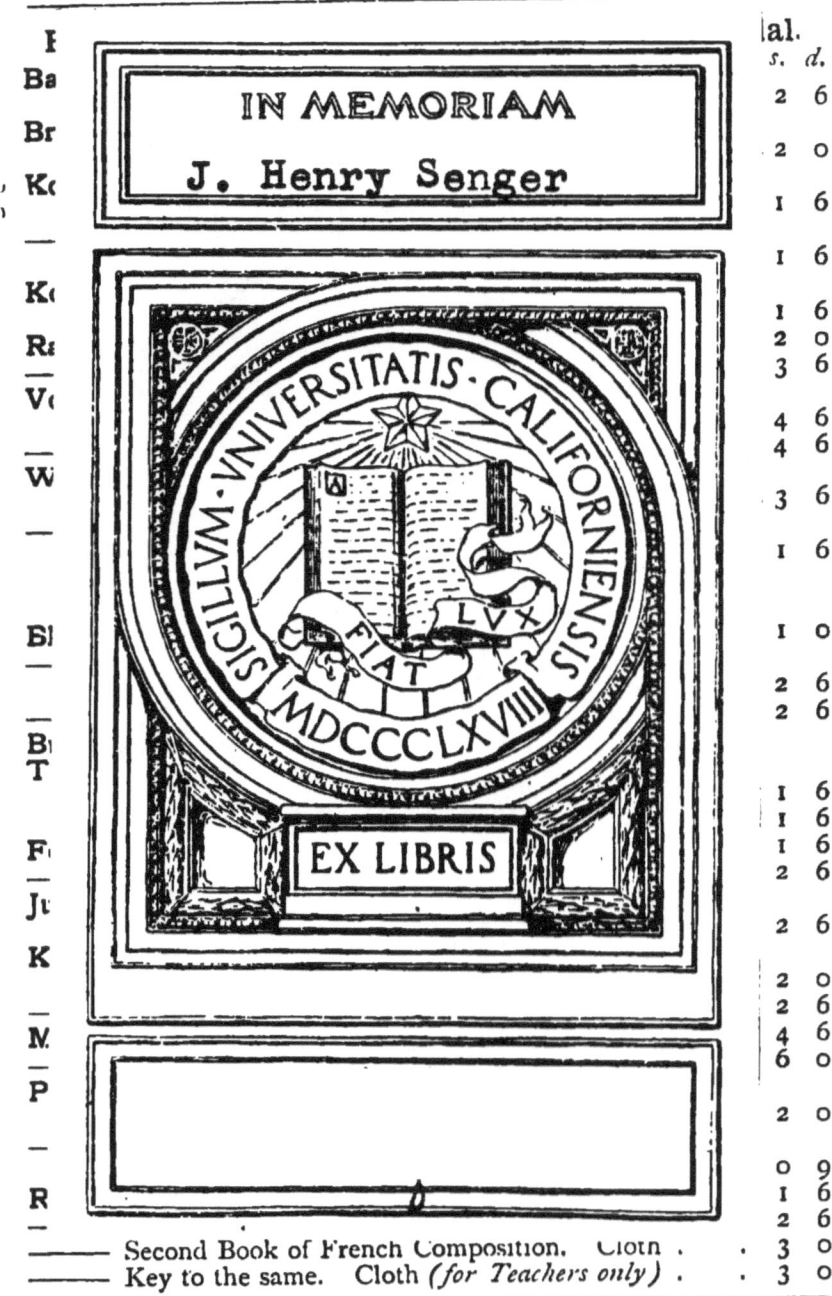

Librairie HACHETTE & Cie

ITALIAN WORKS.

Grammars and Dialogues.

	s.	d.
Dialogues Français-Italiens. Cloth	3	0
English and Italian Dialogues *(in preparation)*.		
Perini, Italian Conversation Grammar.	5	0
Sauer, Italian Conversation Grammar.	5	0
——— Key to the same	2	0

Readers.

Biblioteca Italiana. Edited with Notes and Vocabulary for use in Schools and for Private Students by Rev. A. C. CLAPIN, M.A. Price per Volume, Paper covers . 1 0

    Alfieri, Vittorio, Oreste. Tragedia in cinque atti.
    Carcano, Giulio, La Madre e il Figlio. Novello.
    Carcano, Giulio, Memorie d'un Fanciullo. Il Capellano della Rovella. Novello.
    Goldoni, Carlo, Il Burbero benefico. Commedia in tre atti in prosa.
    Goldoni, Carlo, Un Curioso Accidente. Commedia in tre atti in prosa.
    Goldoni, Carlo, Il Vero amico. Commedia in tre atti in prosa.
    Maffei, Scipione, Merope. Tragedia in cinque atti.

Dante, L'Enfer Ier Chant, Texte Italien, avec des notes en français. Cart 0 10
——— ——— Le même. Avec 2 traductions françaises. Cart 1 0
Ferri, Morceaux choisis des Classiques italiens. Avec notes en français. Cart 2 0
Manzoni, I Promessi Sposi. Texte italien. Cloth . 2 6
Pellico, Le Mie Prigioni. Adapted for English Schools, with Notes. Cloth 1 6
Perini, The First Chapter of I Promessi Sposi, with an English Interlinear Translation. Cloth . . . 2 6
——— La Clemenza di Tito, by Pietro Metastasio, with an English Interlinear Translation. Cloth . . . 2 6
——— First Italian Reading Book in Prose and Poetry, with rules for the pronunciation of the Italian Language, Hints on Italian Versification, and an Accented Vocabulary of all the words contained in the text. Cloth . 1 6
Tasse, La Gerusalemme liberata. Texte italien expurgé. Paper covers . . . , ... 2 6

Dictionaries.

Bermingham, New Dictionary of the English and Italian Languages. 2 parts in 1 Vol., Cloth . . . 6 0
Caccia and Ferrari, Grand Dictionnaire Italien-Français et Français-Italien. 1 Vol., large 8vo., Half-bound . 25 0

18, King William Street, Charing Cross.

Librairie HACHETTE & Cie

SPANISH WORKS.

Grammars, Conversations, and Idioms.

	s.	d.
First Spanish Book. Grammar, Conversation and Translation. With a list of words to be committed to memory and full Vocabulary. Based upon Hugo's Simplified System for learning Spanish. Cloth	2	0
———— Key to the same. Limp cloth.	1	6
First Steps in Spanish Idioms. An alphabetical list of Idioms, explanatory Notes and Examination Papers. By Professor EDOUARDO TOLRÁ, and A. M. BOWER, Ph.D. Cloth	2	0
———— Key to the same. Limp cloth.	1	6
Hugo's Spanish Simplified. A Simplified System for learning Spanish. Cloth	2	0
Conversations. English-Spanish. *(In preparation.)* Cloth	1	6
Dialogues Français-Espagnols. Cloth	3	0
Sauer, Spanish Conversation Grammar. Cloth	5	0
———— Key to the same	2	0

Dictionaries.

	s.	d.
Bustamente, English-Spanish and Spanish-English Dictionary, in 2 Vols. Cloth	6	0
Fonseca, Dictionnaire Français-Espagnol, et Espagnol-Français, Cloth	10	0
Lopez & Bensley, New Dictionary of the Spanish and English Languages. English-Spanish, Spanish-English in 1 Vol., about 1,400 pages. Half-bound	20	0
Salva, Dictionnaire Français-Espagnol, et Espagnol-Français, in 1 Vol. Cloth	6	0
Scholl, Phraseological Dictionary of Commercial Correspondence. English-Spanish. Cloth	12	0

VOLAPÜK.

	s.	d.
The Complete Grammar of Volapük with Exercises and 2 Complete Vocabularies of about 5,000 Words, by Prof. I. HENRY HARRISON. New Edition. Cloth	2	6

18, King William Street, Charing Cross.

FIRST STEPS

IN

GERMAN IDIOMS

CONTAINING

An Alphabetical List of Idioms
Explanatory Notes and Examination Papers

BY

The Rev. A. L. BECKER,

Member of the Philological Society of London,
Author of the "First German Book" in the same Series.

HACHETTE & Co.

LONDON: 18, King William Street, Charing Cross
PARIS: 79, Boulevard Saint-Germain
BOSTON: Carl Schoenhof
1891

PREFACE.

CONSIDERING that "Idioms" are *peculiarities*, I have tried, in adopting the widest sense of the word, to give a fair selection of them for the beginner who has learnt at least the accidence, and the fundamental rules of construction. My mother-tongue is extremely rich in peculiar words and expressions, the rendering of which often presents considerable difficulty, even to the more experienced. The short notes and the comparative hints, together with frequent quotations from German standard authors, will, I trust, make the book both useful and interesting. To secure originality, I have abstained from consulting any work of the kind published anywhere. The exercises at the end of the book, being short and easy, will tend to fix the idioms on the mind. The spelling is the recently introduced official one, in use in German schools, and adopted by the German press.

I might be told that these things had better be learnt in Germany, but I answer that experience has taught me that during a short residence of a year or two in that country, idioms are, as a rule, *not* thoroughly grasped, owing to the defective training most learners have had before entering on conversational practice.

No foreigner ever "*picked up*" grammatical and idiomatic German from merely hearing it spoken or speaking it himself, without a conscientious and indefatigable corrector, and good text-books at his elbow. The better prepared he sets out for the continent, the more rapid will be his progress, and he will thus save both time and money.

May this companion volume to M. Bué's "First Steps in French Idioms" be as kindly received as was the "First German Book" ten years ago. The latter has now reached nine editions.

IPSWICH, *August*, 1891.

A. L. BECKER.

FIRST STEPS
IN
GERMAN IDIOMS.

A.

A.—Wer A sagt, muß auch B sagen.	He who begins a thing, must go on with it.
Ab. — Das Dampfboot fährt stromab. (1)	The steamboat is going down the river.
Abc.—Das sind ABC-schützen.	They are mere beginners.
Das geschieht ab und zu. (2)	That happens occasionally.
Aber.—Der Mensch hat immer ein Aber.	The fellow has always some objection or other.
Die Sache hat ein Aber.	There is a *but* in this business.
Abfertigen.—Wir haben einen Boten an ihn abgefertigt. (3)	We despatched a messenger to him.
Er hat ihn kurz abgefertigt.	He set him down.

B

Abholen. — Holen Sie mich um halb vier Uhr ab.

Come and call for me at half past three.

Abkommen. — Um von der Sache abzukommen, bezahlte ich die Rechnung.

To put an end to the matter, I paid the bill.

Der Hund ist von der Fährte abgekommen.

The dog has lost his scent.

Ich konnte nicht eine Minute abkommen.

I could not spare a minute.

Also. — Mit dem hat es also seine Richtigkeit. (4)

That is true then.

Sie haben also Berlin verlassen?

So you have left Berlin?

An. — London liegt an der Themse. (5)

London lies on the Thames.

Das Gemälde hängt an der Wand.

The picture hangs against the wall.

Ein Weib saß am Feuer.

A woman sat near the fire.

Es ist an der Zeit zu gehen.

It is about time to go.

An und für sich ist es wahr.

In the abstract it is true.

Du solltest dir ein Beispiel an ihr nehmen.

You ought to profit by her example.

Es ist an Ihnen.	It is your turn.
Das geht Sie nichts an.	That does not regard you.
Was geht Sie das an?	What do you want to meddle with that for?
Anhaben. — Niemand kann ihm etwas anhaben.	Nobody can lay anything to his charge.
Ansicht. — Ich habe mir schöne Ansichten von Paris gekauft.	I bought beautiful views of Paris.
Meiner Ansicht nach ist er im Irrtum.	In my opinion he is mistaken.
Das sind Ansichten.	These are matters of opinion.
Ansichtig. — Wir wurden der Insel ansichtig.	We caught sight of the island.
Anker. — Der Dampfer liegt vor Anker.	The steamer is riding at anchor.
Die Brigantine trieb vor Anker.	The brigantine dragged her anchor.
Anklang. — Seine Rede fand keinen Anklang.	His speech was not liked.
Anlaß. — Dazu hatte ich keinen Anlaß.	I had no cause for it.
Anlassen (sich). — Der Knabe läßt sich gut an.	That is a hopeful boy.

Das Wetter läßt sich zum Regen an.	It looks like rain.
Er hat ihn scharf angelassen.	He has given him a sharp rebuke.
Anstand. — Das Mädchen hat keinen Anstand.	That girl has no manners.
Das hat keinen Anstand.	There is no objection.
Auch. — Er ist ein Deutscher; ich auch. (6)	He is a German; so am I.
Er geht nicht; ich auch nicht.	He is not going; nor am I.
Ist es auch so?	Is it really so?
Auch wahr, antwortete mein Bruder.	True, answered my brother.
Hast Du den Brief auch abgegeben, Karl?	Are you sure you delivered the letter, Charles?
Das ist auch wahr.	To be sure.
Auch recht.	I do not mind.
Das ist auch gar zu schlimm.	Why, that is too bad.
Auf. — Auf, laßt uns gehen!	Come, let us go!
Zählen Sie von unten auf.	Count, beginning from below.
Er ging im Garten auf und ab.	He was taking a turn in the garden.

Ich habe das Zimmer auf vier Wochen gemietet.	I have taken the room for four weeks.
Die Sonne ging um drei Viertel auf vier Uhr auf.	The sun rose at a quarter to four.
Sonne, Mond und Sterne **gehen** auf; die Menschen **stehen** auf.	Sun, moon and stars rise; man gets up.
Der Arzt kam um ein Viertel auf zwölf an.	The doctor arrived at a quarter-past eleven.
Meine Schwester war auf dem Ball.	My sister was at the ball.
Er kam auf die Minute.	He came to the minute.
Auf seine Bitte ging ich dahin.	At his request, I went there.
Wie heißt das auf deutsch?	What is this called in German?
Ich werde auf jeden Fall morgen abreisen.	I shall start to-morrow at all events.
Aus. — Die Schule ist aus.	School is over.
Mit der Geschichte ist es aus.	That matter has come to nothing.
Aus den Augen, aus dem Sinn.	Out of sight, out of mind.
Er that es aus Neid.	He did it from envy.

Der Herr kömmt aus München.	The gentleman comes from Munich.
Das will mir nicht aus dem Sinn.	I cannot forget it.
Er las uns ein Märchen aus alten Zeiten vor.	He read to us a fairy tale of ancient times.
Dieser Tisch ist aus Eichenholz.	This table is oak.
Auswendig. — Wenn Du es auswendig gelernt hast, warum weißt Du es nicht auswendig?	If you have learnt it by heart, why do you not know it by heart?
Auszug. — Haben Sie vom Auszuge der Truppen gehört?	Have you heard of the departure of the troops?
Ich mache einen Auszug.	I am writing an extract.

B.

Bald. — Bald wäre ich gefallen.	I had nearly fallen.
Das Ding ist bald gethan.	That is easily done.
Bald kommt er zu uns, bald gehen wir zu ihm.	Sometimes he comes to see us, at other times we go to see him.
Das geschah bald nachher.	That happened soon after.

Bar. — Ich zahle stets bar. (7) — I always pay cash.

Hundert Mark bar. — A hundred marks down.

Das ist eine bare Erdichtung. — That is a downright fiction.

Bär. — Er hat ihm einen Bären aufgebunden. (8) — He imposed upon him.

Bart. — Was brummt er in den Bart? — What is he mumbling?

Sie streiten sich um des Kaisers Bart. (9) — They are disputing about mere trifles.

Bedenken. — Er trug kein Bedenken. — He made no scruple.

Er bedachte sich eines Bessern. — He thought better of it.

Bedeuten. — Es hat nichts zu bedeuten. — It does not signify.

Was soll das bedeuten? — What is the meaning of that?

Bedienen (sich). — Bitte bedienen Sie sich. (10) — Pray, help yourself.

Befehlen. — Was befehlen Sie? (11) — What would you have?

Ich habe Austern befohlen. — I have ordered some oysters.

Befinden (das). — Wie steht es mit Ihrem Befinden? — How is your health?

Herr Müller erkundigte sich nach meines Vaters Befinden. — Mr. Müller inquired after my father's health.

Befinden (sich). — Wie befinden Sie sich? (12) — How do you do?

Er befindet sich im Irrtum. — He is labouring under a mistake.

Begreifen. — Das kann ich nicht begreifen. (13) — I cannot comprehend that.

Ich begreife nicht, warum er nicht gekommen ist. — I cannot see why he did not come.

Begriff. — Das geht über Wilhelms Begriffe. — That is beyond William's capacity.

Wir waren im Begriffe uns einzuschiffen. — We were about to embark.

Begriffen sein. — Wir sind auf der Reise begriffen. (14) — We are on a journey.

Die Gesandten waren in Unterhandlungen begriffen. — The ambassadors were in treaty.

Behalten. — Ich habe es gelernt, aber ich kann es nicht behalten. — I have learnt it, but I cannot remember it.

Bei. — Bei gutem Wetter gehen wir aus. (15) — In fine weather we go out.

Ist er bei sich? — Is he in his right senses?

Bei aller Vorsicht verliert er doch immer.	With all his caution, he is constantly losing.
Bei meiner Ehre!	Upon my honour!
Beistimmen.—Ich stimme Ihnen bei.	I agree with you.
Bekleiden.—Wer ein Amt bekleidet, heißt ein Beamter.	He who holds office is called an official.
Betreffen.—Der Dieb wurde auf der That betroffen.	The thief was caught in the act.
Was uns betrifft, werden wir nichts in der Sache thun.	As for us, we shall do nothing in the matter.
Betrieb.—Das Bergwerk ist im Betrieb. (16)	The mine is being worked.
Bett.—Er mußte das Bett hüten.	He had to keep his bed.
Blank.—Er ging mit blankem Degen auf ihn los. (17)	He rushed on him with his sword drawn.
Blau.—Die Arbeiter machten blauen Montag. (18)	The workmen were idle on Monday.
Der Kerl schwatzt immer ins Blaue. (19)	The fellow is constantly talking idle rubbish.
Blut.—Du siehst wie Milch und Blut aus.	You are looking all roses and lilies.

Du bist noch ein junges Blut.	You are still young.
Bockshorn.—Die Jungen ließen sich ins Bockshorn jagen. (20)	The youngsters were intimidated.
Bodensee.—Hast Du je den Bodensee gesehen? (21)	Have you ever seen the lake of Constance?
Bohren.—Das Kriegsschiff wurde in den Grund gebohrt.	The man of war was sunk.
Brand.—Das Magazin geriet in Brand.	The stores caught fire.
Der heiße und der kalte Brand sind sehr gefährlich.	Gangrene and mortification are very dangerous.
Bringen.—Was bringen Sie Neues? (22)	What is the news?
Dieser Gelehrte kann sein Wissen nicht an den Mann bringen.	This scholar cannot utilize his learning.
Dieser junge Mann bringt es nicht weit.	This young man does not get on.
Er hat es zu nichts gebracht.	He did not get on.
Die Sonne bringt alles ans Licht.	The sun brings everything to light.
Die Waren wurden in Sicherheit gebracht.	The goods were placed in safety.

Sie kann es nicht übers Herz bringen.	She cannot find it in her heart.
Der Verbrecher hat sich ums Leben gebracht.	The criminal committed suicide.
Man hat ihn heute zu Grabe gebracht.	He was buried to-day.
Bruder. — Heinrich ist ein lustiger Bruder.	Henry is a jolly good fellow.
Busen. — Albert ist mein Busenfreund. (23)	Albert is my intimate friend.
Neapel liegt am Meerbusen gleichen Namens.	Naples lies on the bay of the same name.

D.

Da. — Die Schildwache rief „Wer da?" (24)	The sentry shouted, "Who goes there?"
Mein Herr ist nicht da.	My master is out.
Dafür. — Ich stehe dafür. (25)	I warrant you.
Dagegen. — Ich habe nichts dagegen.	I do not object to that.
Daheim. — Er ist im Deutschen nicht daheim.	He is not conversant with German.
Dahinter. — Es ist nichts dahinter.	There is nothing in it.
Damalig. — Der damalige Direktor war ein Ehrenmann.	The headmaster of that time was a man of honour.

Damit.—Damit ist es aus. / It is all up with it.

Damit ist alles gesagt. / There is an end of it.

Heraus damit! / Out with it!

Hinein damit! / Put it in there!

Danach.—Ich frage nichts danach. / I do not care.

Kurz danach kam er. / He came shortly after.

Danach es sich trifft. / As it happens.

Danieder.—Er liegt am Fieber danieder. / He is laid up with fever.

Dann und wann.—Er schreibt mir dann und wann. / He writes to me now and then.

Daran.—Es liegt mir nichts daran. / I do not care.

Er hat daran glauben müssen. / He died.

Die Leute sind gut daran. / These people are well off.

Ich weiß nicht, wie ich mit ihm daran bin. / I do not know what to think of him.

Daran bin ich nicht Schuld. / It is not my fault.

Ich zweifle nicht daran. / I do not doubt it.

Darauf.—Er gab mir die Hand darauf. / He gave me his hand upon it.

Er ist sehr darauf versessen. / He is very much bent upon it.

Wie sind Sie darauf verfallen?	How did you hit upon it?
Den Tag darauf kam die Nachricht.	The day after news came.
Daraus.—Daraus wird nichts.	That cannot be.
Darein. — Sie müssen sich darein finden.	You must try to get reconciled to it.
Die Regierung sollte sich darein legen.	Government ought to interfere.
Darüber. — Man klagt darüber.	They are complaining of it.
Darüber bin ich hinaus.	I am above that.
Darunter. — Was verstehen Sie darunter?	What do you mean by that?
Da geht es darunter und darüber.	Things are running wild.
(usually shortened into brunter und brüber.)	
Dasig. — Der dasige Pfarrer ist gestorben. (26)	The rector of that place died.
Dawider. — Ich habe nichts dawider.	I have nothing against it.
Dazu.—Es gehört viel Geld dazu.	That wants a deal of money.
Dazumal gab es viele Bettler.	At that time there were a great many beggars.

Decke.—Ich strecke mich nach der Decke.	I accommodate myself to circumstances.
Decken. — Die Magd deckt den Tisch.	The servant is laying the table.
Derartig. — Derartiges Betragen ist strafbar.	Such behaviour is punishable.
Dergleichen. —Dergleichen findet man jetzt nicht mehr.	You no longer find the like.
Er that nicht dergleichen.	He pretended not to be aware.
Desto besser. — Desto besser, sagte der Lehrer. (27)	All the better, said the master.
Deutsch. — Lassen Sie mich mit Ihnen deutsch reden. (28)	Let me be plain with you.
Dienen. — Womit kann ich Ihnen dienen?	What is your pleasure?
Damit ist mir nicht gedient.	That will never answer my purpose.
Ding.—Gut Ding will Weile haben.	Things take time to be done properly.
Was für ein einfältig Ding Du bist!	What a silly thing you are!
Doch. — Ich bin jetzt wieder gesund; doch muß ich mich sehr in acht nehmen.	I am now well again, but I must take very great care of myself.

Gieb mir doch das Buch!	Give me the book, pray!
Sie kommen doch?	You will come, I hope.
Weißt Du es denn nicht?	Do you really not know?
Doch, ich weiß es.	Yes, I do.
Sage mir's doch! Nicht doch.	Do tell me! No, certainly not.
Dreißiger. — Er ist ein Dreißiger.	He is between 30 and 40 years old.
Dritt. — Der Fisch wiegt dritthalb Pfund. (29)	The fish weighs two pounds and a half.
Mein Vetter wohnt im drittletzten Hause. (30)	My cousin lives in the last house but two.
Die drittletzte Silbe eines Wortes heißt auf lateinisch "ante-penultima."	The last syllable but two of a word is called in Latin "ante-penultima."
Durch. — Er spielte den ganzen Sommer durch.	He played through the whole summer.
Durchaus nicht. — Sie wollte durchaus nicht nachgeben.	She would not yield in the least.
Durchkommen. — Der Kandidat ist im Examen durchgekommen.	The candidate has passed his examination.
Dürfen. — Darf ich spielen? (31)	May I play?
Darf ich mich darauf verlassen?	May I rely on it?

E.

Das dürfte nicht schwer sein.	That ought not to be difficult.
Wer dürfte an seiner Redlichkeit zweifeln.	Who would doubt his honesty.

Eben.—Ich gehe ebendahin. (32) — I am going to the same place.

Den eben suche ich. — He is the very man I am looking for.

Er war eben hier. — He was here just now.

Ei.—Ei, das ist ja herrlich. — Why, that is really splendid.

Ei, so geh doch! (33) — Go, I say!

Eigen.—Er ist ein eigner Kauz. (34) — He is a rum fellow.

Eigentlich hätte ich es nicht thun sollen. — Really, I ought not to have done it.

Eigentlich (35) habe ich das Buch nicht gelesen. — To tell you the truth, I have not read the book.

Eile.—Ich hatte Eile. (36) — I was in a hurry.

Ein.—Jahr aus Jahr ein. (37) — All the year round.

Ich weiß nicht wo aus, wo ein. — I do not know what to do.

Einerlei.—Es ist mir einerlei. — It is all the same to me.

Einfall.—Das war ein witziger Einfall. — That was an ingenious idea.

Einfallen. — Mir fällt was ein. — Something strikes me.

Einladen.—Ich bin ein für allemal eingeladen. — I have a general invitation.

Einmaleins.—Der kleine Wilhelm lernt das Einmaleins. — Little William is learning his multiplication tables.

Einnehmend. — Der Arzt ist ein Mann von einnehmendem Äußern. — The doctor is a man of prepossessing appearance.

Einrücken. — Ich ließ die Anzeige dreimal in das Tageblatt einrücken. (38) — I had the advertisement inserted 3 times in the daily paper.

Eins.—Es ist halb eins. — It is 12.30.
Mir ist alles eins. — It is all one to me.

Einschläfern. (39) — Das Opium ist ein einschläferndes Mittel. — Opium is a soporific.
Er ließ sich einschläfern. — He allowed himself to be deluded with vain hopes.

Einschreiben. — Lassen Sie den Brief einschreiben? — Are you getting the letter registered?

c

Einschränken. — Wir müssen uns einschränken.	We must retrench our expenses.
Eintragen. — Das trägt nicht viel ein.	That does not yield much profit.
Eintritt. — Auf der Thür stand „Freier Eintritt!"	There was this notice on the door, "Admission Free."
Einverstanden.	Agreed.
Einzahl. — Das Wort kömmt nur in der Einzahl vor.	That word only occurs in the singular number.
Einzahlen. — Ich habe soeben hundert Mark für Dich eingezahlt.	I have just deposited 100 marks for you.
Eisen. — Man muß das Eisen schmieden, weil (40) es warm ist.	You must strike the iron whilst it is hot.
Not bricht Eisen.	Necessity knows no law.
Empfehlen. — Ich empfehle mich Ihnen.	Good day.
Empfehlen Sie mich Ihrer Frau Mutter.	Give my kind regards to your mother.
Empfehlung. — Meine Empfehlung!	My compliments!
Der junge Mann hat Empfehlungsbriefe an den Gesandten.	The young man has letters of introduction to the ambassador.

Entgegengehen. — Wir gingen unserem Freunde entgegen. (41)
We went to meet our friend.

Erbitten. — Sie läßt sich nicht erbitten. (42)
She is inexorable.

Erfahrung. — Wir werden es schon in Erfahrung bringen.
We are sure to ascertain it.

Ergreifend. — Ich las eine ergreifende Geschichte. (43)
I read a thrilling story.

Erholen. — Ich habe mir bei meinem Advokaten Rats erholt.
I got advice from my lawyer.

Haben Sie sich von Ihrer Anstrengung erholt?
Have you recovered from your exertion?

Erlogen. — Das ist erlogen.
That is a lie.

Erst. — Es ist erst halb eins.
It is only half past twelve.

Der Hauptmann war erst dreißig Jahre alt.
The captain was only thirty years old.

Wäre ich nur erst zu Hause!
If I were but at home!

Hätten Sie die dicken Mauern erst gesehen!
If you had but seen the thick walls!

Er kommt erst um sieben Uhr.
He will not be here before seven.

Nun erst fiel es mir ein.	Not till then it occurred to me.
Ich habe ihn erst recht liebgewonnen.	I have got more fond of him than ever.
Es.—Ich bin es or ich bin's.	It is I.
Sind Sie es?	Is it you?
Es lebe die Königin!	Long live the Queen!
Es singt jemand.	Somebody is singing.
Diese Leute haben es gut.	These people are well off.
Er meint es gut mit Dir.	He means well by you.
Etwas.—Das will etwas sagen.	That is saying a great deal.
Eule.—Eulen nach Athen tragen. (44)	To carry coals to Newcastle.
Examen.—Er hat sein Examen bestanden.	He passed his examination.
Er ist im Examen durchgefallen.	He was "plucked."
Extra.—Es steht im Extrablatt.	It is in the supplement (paper).
Extrem.—Extreme berühren sich. (45)	Extremes meet.

F.

Fabrik.—Wir besuchten die Papierfabrik. (46) — We paid a visit to the paper mill.

Die Fabrikarbeiter waren unzufrieden. — The factory-men were dissatisfied.

Birmingham und Manchester sind Fabrikstädte. — Birmingham and Manchester are manufacturing towns.

Wir liefern Ihnen diese Ware zum Fabrikpreis. — We supply you these goods at first cost.

Fach.—Dazu braucht es einen Mann von Fach. — For *that* a professional man is required.

Der Herr ist ein Gelehrter von Fach. (47) — The gentleman is a professed scholar.

Fahne.—Mit fliegenden Fahnen. — With flying colours.

Fahr.—Die Fahrzeit und der Fahrpreis stehen auf dem Fahrplan. — The time of departure and the fare are on the time-table.

Fahren.—Die Dampfschiffe fahren regelmäßig. (48) — The steamers are running regularly.

Der Metzger fährt zu schnell. — The butcher drives too fast.

Der Fürst fuhr mit Vieren aus. — The Prince drove out in a coach and four.

Wo fahren Sie hin? Ich fahre nach Köln. — Where are you booked for? For Cologne.

Der Schnellzug fährt um sechs Uhr fünfzig ab.	The fast train leaves at 6.50.
Es fährt sich angenehm.	This is nice travelling.
Da möchte man aus der Haut fahren.	It is enough to drive one mad.
Fall.—Hochmut kommt vor dem Falle, wie das Sprichwort sagt.	Pride goes before, and shame follows after, as the proverb has it.
Ich setze den Fall.	I suppose.
Nötigenfalls bezahle ich die Kosten. (49)	If need be, I will pay the costs.
Im besten Falle wird es noch schwer genug gehen.	It will still go hard enough at best.
Sollten Sie je in den Fall kommen.	Should you ever have the chance.
Das wird er auf keinen Fall thun.	He will do it on no account.
Haben Sie allenfalls den Schlüssel in der Tasche?	Do you happen to have the key in your pocket?
Fallen.—Es lag ein gefallenes Pferd am Wege.	A dead horse was lying by the road side.
Du bist nicht auf den Kopf gefallen.	You are no fool.
Er fiel dem Pferde in die Zügel.	He seized the horse's bridle.

Man muß den Leuten nicht in das Wort fallen.	One ought not to interrupt people.
Ostern fiel dieses Jahr auf den neun und zwanzigsten März.	Easter happened to be this year on the 29th of March.
Es fielen mehrere Schüsse.	Several shots were fired.
Das Gehen fällt den alten Leuten oft schwer.	Old people often walk with difficulty.
Das Land ist sehr im Werte gefallen.	Land has very much fallen in value.
Fällen. — Der Richter fällte das Urteil. (50)	The judge gave sentence.
Fällig. — Der Zins ist fällig.	The interest is due.
Der Zug ist fällig.	The train is due.
Falsch. — Das ist falsch.	That is wrong.
Der Thaler war falsch.	The thaler was counterfeit.
Die Schauspielerin trägt falsche Diamanten.	The actress wears sham diamonds.
Sie singt falsch. (51)	She is singing out of tune.
Familie. — Der Arzt hat eine große Familie.	The doctor has a large family.
Fassen. — Ich muß mich zuerst fassen.	I must first collect my thoughts.

Ich hatte mich nicht darauf gefaßt gemacht.	I was not prepared for it.
Fassen Sie sich kurz.	Be brief.
Das kann ein Kind nicht fassen.	A child cannot grasp that.
Faust.—Das reimt sich wie die Faust aufs Auge. (52)	Why, that has neither rhyme nor reason.
Er that es auf eigene Faust.	He did it on his own responsibility.
Im Mittelalter herrschte oft das Faustrecht.	In the middle ages club law often reigned supreme.
Fehl.—Der Jäger schoß fehl.	The sportsman missed the mark.
Fehlen. — Gefehlt, mein Junge!	Wrong, my boy!
Daran soll es nicht fehlen.	Let that make no difference.
Was fehlt Ihnen?	What is the matter with you?
Es fehlt mir nichts.	There is nothing the matter with me.
Feiern. — Die Arbeiter feiern. (53)	The workmen are having a holiday.
Fein. (54)—Das ist ein feines Gewebe.	That is a delicate texture.
Er ist ein feingebildeter Mann.	He is an accomplished gentleman.

Sei mir fein klug.	Mind, be wise.
Feind.—Der böse Feind hat das gethan.	The demon has done that.
Feind.—Er ist ihm feind. (55)	He is his enemy.
Feld.—Er ist noch nie im Felde gewesen.	He has not seen service as yet.
Das Heer rückt ins Feld.	The army is taking the field.
Wie viele Regimenter kann der Feind ins Feld stellen?	How many regiments can the enemy bring into the field?
Fell.—Der Kerl hat ein dickes Fell. (56)	The fellow is thick-skinned.
Ferien.—Unsere Ferien dauern sechs Wochen. (57)	Our holidays last six weeks.
Feuer.—Das Haus stand in Feuer.	The house was on fire.
Er spie Feuer und Flammen.	He was fretting and fuming.
Die Hexe wurde zum Feuer verurteilt.	The witch was condemned to the stake.
Fiaker.—Holen Sie mir einen Fiaker. (58)	Fetch a cab for me.
Fidel.—Max ist ein fideles Haus. (59)	Max is a jolly fellow.

Fidibus.—Kellner, geben Sie mir einen Fidibus! (60) — Waiter, give me a lighter.

Filiale.—Die Rheinische Bank hat hier eine Filiale. — The Rhenish Bank has a branch establishment here.

Fischbein.—Das Fischbein ist biegsam. (61) — Whalebone is flexible.

Fischen.—Er fischt im Trüben. — He is fishing in troubled waters.

Flächeninhalt. — Der Flächeninhalt von Texas ist größer als der von Frankreich. (62) — The area of Texas is larger than that of France.

Flau.—Der Handel ist flau. (63) — Trade is dull.

Flause.— Das ist nur eine Flause. — That is only a false pretence.

Fleck.—Da haben Sie den rechten Fleck getroffen. — There you have struck home.

Der Mann hat Herz und Kopf am rechten Fleck. (64) — The man has a stout heart and clear head.

Flecken.—Dieser Flecken hat nur achtzehnhundert Einwohner. — This small country town has but 1800 inhabitants.

Fleisch. — Fleisch und Blut hält das nicht aus.
Human nature cannot stand that.

Fliege. — Zwei Fliegen mit einem Schlage treffen.
To kill two birds with one stone.

Flott. — Er ist ein flotter Kamerad. (65)
He is a gay fellow.

Dort geht es flott her.
They are living a jolly life there.

Flucht. — Wir haben sieben Zimmer in einer Flucht.
We have seven rooms on one flat.

Flüchtig. — Das ist flüchtige Arbeit.
That is desultory work.

Flurschütz. — Er wurde von einem Flurschützen angehalten. (66)
He was stopped by a rural guard.

Flut. — Die Flut kam eben als wir abfuhren.
The tide was just coming in, when we started.

Fort. — Fort mit Dir!
Be gone!

Er singt in einem fort.
He sings incessantly.

Sie waren schon fort.
They were gone already.

Mußt Du schon fort?
Must you be going already?

Damit kommst Du nicht fort.
That will not serve your purpose.

Frage.—Davon ist jetzt nicht die Frage. (67)	That is out of the question now.
Das ist ein Fragewort.	That is an interrogative particle.
Hieher gehört ein Fragezeichen.	There ought to be a note of interrogation here.
Fraglich.—Der fragliche Umstand.	The circumstance in question.
Fragselig.—Du bist ein fragseliges Kind. (68)	You are a child fond of asking questions.
Freitag. — Karfreitag ist der Freitag vor Ostern. (68A)	Good Friday is the Friday before Easter.
Fremd.—Das war meiner Absicht fremd.	That was remote from my purpose.
Fremde (die).—Er lebt in der Fremde. (69)	He lives abroad.
Er kam erst kürzlich aus der Fremde.	He only returned from abroad a short while ago.
Fressen (70). — Vogel, friß oder stirb.	There is no other remedy.
Frieren. — Friert es Dich?	Are you cold?
Es friert mich an die Hände.	My hands are cold.
Es war Stein und Bein gefroren.	There was an extremely hard frost.

Frisch. — Man fing den Taschendieb auf frischer That.
The pickpocket was caught in the very act.

Frohn (71).— Die Bauern mußten früher oft Frohndienste leisten.
The peasants had formerly often to perform compulsory labour.

Frohnvogt heißt Aufseher über Frohnarbeiter.
"Frohnvogt" means overseer of a forced labour gang.

Frohnleichnamsfest.
Corpus Christi Festival.

Fromm. — Das ist nur ein frommer Wunsch.
That is only a vain wish.

Frommen. — Das frommt ihm nicht.
That is of no profit to him.

Frösteln.—Mich fröstelt.
I feel rather cold.

Früh. — Kommen Sie morgen früh.
Come early to-morrow morning.

Ich arbeite morgens früh.
I am at work early in the morning.

Führen.—Er will immer das Wort führen.
He always wants to be spokesman.

Fülle.—Sie haben Geld die Hülle und Fülle.
They have money in abundance.

Fund.—Wir haben einen Fund gethan.
We have found something.

Funkelnagelneu.(72)— Das ist ja funkelnagelneu!
Why, that is spick and span!

Für.—An und für sich ist es wahr. — In the abstract it is true.

Fürs erste sind Sie nicht reich genug. — In the first place you are not rich enough.

Furore.—Der Tonkünstler hat Furore gemacht. (73) — The musician has created quite a sensation.

Fürwort. — Wir lernen jetzt die deutschen Fürwörter. — We are learning the German pronouns now.

Fuß. — Der Stock ist vier Fuß lang. (74) — The stick is four feet long.

Ich will dem Jungen Füße machen. — I will make the boy find his legs.

Die Kriegsgefangenen werden auf freien Fuß gesetzt. — The prisoners of war are being released.

Wir stehen auf freundlichem Fuße mit einander. — We are on friendly terms with each other.

Die Familie lebt auf großem Fuße. (75) — The family are living in great style.

Wir gehen zu Fuße. — We walk on foot.

Er wurde zum Fußkusse zugelassen. — He was allowed to kiss the Pope's feet.

Er gab dem Schurken einen Fußtritt. — He gave the scoundrel a kick.

Futter. — Die Reiterei hat Futter gefaßt. (76) — The cavalry have been foraging.

Der Mantel hat ein seidenes Futter. — The cloak has a silk lining.

G.

Gabelfrühstück. — In Frankreich ist das Gabelfrühstück gewöhnlich zwischen zehn und zwölf Uhr zu haben. (77)

In France meat breakfast is generally to be had between 10 and 12 o'clock.

Galanterie. — Ist eine Galanteriewarenhandlung in Ihrer Straße?

Is there a fancy articles shop in your street?

Galgen. — Der Mensch sieht wahrhaftig aus als wäre er vom Galgen gefallen.

Why, this fellow looks dead and dug up again.

Galle. — Die Galle lief ihm über. (78)

His anger was up.

Galopp. — Sie ritten bald im kurzen, bald im gestreckten Galopp.

At times they were cantering, and then again they rode at full gallop.

Galoppierend. — Der Kranke hat die galoppierende Schwindsucht.

The patient is in rapid decline.

Gang. — Unser Geschäft ist in vollem Gange.

Our business is at full work.

Ich habe einen Gang zu thun.

I must go out on business.

Das Mittagsmahl bestand aus sechs Gängen.

The dinner consisted of six courses.

Gangbar.—Diese Münze ist hier nicht gangbar. (79)

This coin is not current here.

Das ist eine gangbare Straße.

That is a frequented thoroughfare.

Ganz.— Ich bin ganz allein.

I am quite alone.

Da haben Sie ganz recht.

There you are quite right.

Gar.—Iß, was gar ist; sprich, was wahr ist. (80)

Eat what is cooked, speak what is true.

Ich hatte gar kein Geld mehr.

I had not a bit of money left.

Die Jungen machen es gar zu arg.

The boys are really behaving too badly.

Ganz und gar nicht!

By no means!

Ich bin gar zu froh.

I cannot tell you how glad I am.

Gassenhauer.—Das ist ein gemeiner Gassenhauer. (81)

That is a common street song.

Gast.—Wir müssen ihn zu Gast bitten.

We must invite him to dinner.

Er hat sich selbst zu Gaste geboten.

He has come uninvited.

Ich bin bei meinen Freunden zu Gaste.

I am staying with my friends.

Wollen Sie unser Gast sein?

Will you dine with us?

Geben.—Der Arzt giebt ihm noch zwanzig Jahre.
The doctor thinks he has a chance to live 20 years more.

Es giebt keine Geister.
There are no ghosts.

Die Zeit wird es geben.
Time will show.

Du mußt dir Mühe geben.
You must take pains.

Die Sache wird sich bald geben.
The matter will soon be made up.

Was giebt es da zu lachen?
Why do you laugh there?

Es hat Schläge gegeben.
They came to blows.

Der größte Gelehrte, den es je gegeben hat.
The greatest scholar that ever was.

Gebildet.—Das ist ein Buch für Gebildete. (82)
That is a book for the educated.

Gebunden.—In gebundener Rede ist dieser Ausdruck nicht gebräuchlich.
In poetry this expression is not in use.

Gedächtnis.—Es war meinem Gedächtnisse entfallen.
It had escaped my memory.

Gedanke.—Was bringt Sie auf den Gedanken?
What makes you think so?

Gedanken sind zollfrei.
Opinions are free.

D

Gediegen. — Er ist ein gediegener Mann. (83)	He is a sterling man.
Gefahr. — Sie thun das auf Ihre Gefahr.	You do this at your risk.
Gefallen. — Thun Sie es mir zu Gefallen. (84)	Do it to please me.
Das gefällt mir nicht.	I am not pleased with that.
Ich lebe ihr zum Gefallen.	I humour her.
Gefallen (*verb*). — Das lasse ich mir gefallen.	I agree to that.
Gefällig. — Wenn es Ihnen gefällig ist.	If you please.
Gefälligst. — Kommen Sie gefälligst herein. (85)	Please come in.
Gefällt Ihnen das?	Do you like that?
Gefallsüchtig. — Sie ist gefallsüchtig.	She is a coquette.
Gefängnis. — Er kam ins Gefängnis.	He was sent to prison.
Gegen. — Zehn gegen eins, es gelingt ihm.	Ten to one, he will succeed.
Das ist nichts gegen das, was ich sah.	This is nothing compared with what I saw.
Es kamen gegen acht hundert Mann.	There came about 800 men.

Gegend. — Er wohnt irgendwo in der Gegend. (86)

He lives somewhere in that neighbourhood.

Gehen. — Das geht nicht.

That will not do.

Geht an die Arbeit!

Set to work!

Wie geht es Ihnen?

How are you?

Fritz geht jetzt in das siebenzehnte Jahr.

Fred is now going on for seventeen.

Das geht wahrhaftig über meinen Verstand!

That really passes my comprehension.

Wie geht es mit Ihrer Erkältung?

How is your cold?

Es geht auf Leben und Tod. (87)

It is a matter of life and death.

Gehören. — Dazu gehört ein Haufen Geld.

You want a lot of money for that.

Das gehört nicht hieher. (88)

That is out of place here.

Thun Sie wie es sich gehört.

Do what is proper.

Geige. — Der Himmel hängt ihm voller Geigen. (89)

He sees the bright side of everything.

Geist. — Dieser Wein hat Geist.

This wine is racy.

Der Mensch hat keinen Geist.

He is not an intellectual man.

Goethe und Schiller waren Geister erster Größe.

Goethe and Schiller were master minds.

Sie wurde geisteskrank.	She went mad.
Geistlich.—Er ist in den geistlichen Stand getreten.	He has taken orders.
Geistliche. — Der Geistliche predigt sehr gut. (90)	The clergyman preaches very well.
Geld. — Für Geld und gute Worte.	For love or money.
Ich bin nicht sehr bei Gelde.	I am rather hard up.
Der Herr dort lebt von seinem Gelde.	That gentleman yonder lives upon his income.
Er hat Geld wie Heu. (91)	He is weltering in wealth.
Gelegen.—Es ist nicht viel daran gelegen. (92)	It matters little.
Das kommt uns gerade gelegen.	That just suits us.
Gelegenheit. — Ich werde es bei Gelegenheit thun.	I will do it when an opportunity occurs.
Er lacht bei jeder Gelegenheit.	He laughs on all occasions.
Gelegenheit macht Diebe.	Occasion makes the thief.
Mit welcher Gelegenheit reisen Sie?	By what conveyance do you travel?

Gelegentlich. — Schreiben Sie mir gelegentlich.	Write to me at your own convenience.
Gelten. — Was gelten jetzt die Hopfen? (93)	What is the price of hops now?
Diese Münze gilt in England nicht.	This coin is not current in England.
Was gilts?	What do you bet?
Es gilt!	Done!
Hier gilt kein Aufschub.	Delay will not do here.
Geltung. — Er ist ein Mensch ohne alle Geltung.	He is a man of no account whatever.
Gemäß. — Das ist ganz dem Zwecke gemäß. (94)	This is quite to the purpose.
Gemein. — Der gemeine Menschenverstand sagt dir das.	Common sense tells you that.
Gemüt. — Lassen Sie mich Ihnen das zu Gemüte führen.	Let me impress that on your mind.
Der Mensch hat kein Gemüt.	The fellow has no heart.
Genau. — Sie nehmen es zu genau.	You are too particular.
Er kam mit genauer Not durchs Examen.	He just scraped through his examen.
Geneigt. — Ich glaube, er ist Ihnen geneigt.	I think he is favourably disposed towards you.

Genug. — Es ist übrig genug.
There is more than enough.

Des Lachens genug!
No more laughing!

Genugthuung. — Man darf sich nicht selbst Genugthuung verschaffen.
We are not allowed to take the law in our own hands.

Gerade *(adj. & adv.).* — Der gerade Weg ist der beste. (95)
Honesty is the best policy.

Gehen Sie nur gerade fort.
Just go straight on.

Es ist gerade Mittag.
It is just 12 o'clock.

Geraten. — Gut geratene Kinder sind ein großer Segen. (96)
Well-bred children are a great blessing.

Das Haus gerät in Verfall.
The house is falling to decay.

Er geriet in Schulden.
He got into debts

Sie gerieten in Unruhe.
They took alarm.

Gerede. — Sie kam ins Gerede. (97)
She became the town talk.

Man hat den Mann ins Gerede gebracht.
They slandered the man.

Gericht. — Er wurde vor Gericht gefordert.
He got a summons.

Gerichtlich. — Die Gegner wurden gerichtlich vorgeladen.
The opponents were summoned.

Gern or **gerne.** — Ich reise gern. (98)	I like to travel.
Nehmen Sie es; ich gebe es gern.	Take it; you are welcome to it.
Du bist ein kleiner Gernegroß.	You are a little would-be-great.
Geruch. — Er steht in gutem Geruche.	He has a good character.
Geschäft. — Mein Neffe ist in einem Londoner Geschäfte.	My nephew is in a London business.
Herr Maier hat soeben ein eigenes Geschäft angefangen.	Mr. Maier has just set up for himself.
Das Haus macht große Geschäfte.	The house is doing extensive business.
Geschehen. — Es ist gern geschehen.	You are welcome.
Es geschehe was da wolle!	Come what may!
Gesellschaft. — Wollen Sie mir Gesellschaft leisten?	Will you bear me company?
Wir sind mit ihm in Gesellschaft getreten.	We have entered into partnership with him.
Gesicht. — Das Fräulein hat ein kurzes Gesicht.	The young lady is short-sighted.
Er machte ein langes Gesicht.	He looked disappointed.

Die Jungen schnitten Gesichter.	The youngsters were making faces.
Gespannt. — Sie leben mit einander auf gespanntem Fuße.	They are on bad terms with each other.
Gespött. — Sie trieben ihr Gespött mit ihm.	They made fun of him.
Gesprächig. — Er war sehr gesprächig.	He was very communicative.
Gestalt. — Der Held war schön von Gestalt.	The hero was well made.
Gesund. — Ihr Herr Vater sieht sehr gesund aus.	Your father is looking very well.
Das ist Dir gesund, Du Faullenzer.	That serves you right, you lazy rogue.
Gesundheit. — Wie steht es mit Ihrer Gesundheit?	How is your health?
Man brachte seine Gesundheit aus.	They drank his health.
Gewaltig — Sie irren sich gewaltig.	You are grossly mistaken.
Gewehr. — Die Truppen standen den ganzen Tag unter dem Gewehre.	The troops stood the whole day under arms.
Das Gewehr ab!	Ground arms!
Präsentiert das Gewehr!	Present arms!

Gewitter. — Ein Gewitter steigt auf.	A storm is gathering.
Es steht ein Gewitter am Himmel.	There is a thunderstorm coming on.
Gewohnheit. — Gewohnheit wird zur andern Natur.	Use is second nature.
Giftig. — Das böse Weib wurde sehr giftig.	The mischievous woman got very enraged.
Gleich. — Das Bild sieht Ihrem Bruder sehr gleich.	That is a good likeness of your brother.
Die Festung wurde dem Boden gleich gemacht.	The fortress was levelled to the ground.
Man sollte nicht Gleiches mit Gleichem vergelten.	One ought not to retaliate.
Gleich und Gleich gesellt sich gern.	Birds of a feather flock together.
Er kam gleich nachher.	He came immediately after.
Wer war es doch gleich, der eben hier vorbeiging?	Do tell me, pray, who was it that just now passed here?
Er war gleich bei der Hand.	He was ready at hand.
Glied. — Die Soldaten dürfen nicht aus dem Gliede treten.	Soldiers are not allowed to quit the ranks.

Schließt die Glieder!	Double the file!
Glück.—Glück auf!	Good luck!
Seine Frau hat sein Glück gemacht.	His wife was the making of him.
Mein Vetter that es auf gut Glück.	My cousin did it at a venture.
Jeder ist seines Glückes Schmied.	Everyone is the architect of his own fortune.
Ich wünsche Ihnen Glück zum neuen Jahre.	I wish you a happy New Year.
Sie ist ein Glückskind.	She was born with a silver spoon in her mouth.
Nehmen Sie sich vor Glücksrittern in acht!	Beware of adventurers!
Glücken.—Es ist ihm geglückt.	He succeeded.
Glücklich. — Glücklicherweise geschieht das jetzt nicht mehr.	Fortunately that does not happen any more.
Gnade.—Ich bitte mir das als eine Gnade aus. (99)	I ask this as a favour.
Die Besatzung mußte sich auf Gnade und Ungnade ergeben.	The garrison had to surrender at discretion.
Der Elende kam sehr gnädig davon.	The wretch got off very cheaply.

Gold. — Es ist nicht alles Gold was glänzt.	All is not gold that glitters.
Morgenstunde hat Gold im Munde.	Early to bed and early to rise, makes a man healthy, wealthy, and wise.
Reden ist Silber, Schweigen ist Gold.	Least said soonest mended.
Gönnen. — Ich gönne ihm sein Glück. (100)	I do not grudge him his good fortune.
Gönner. — Der Graf war seines Vaters Freund und Gönner.	The count was his father's friend and patron.
Gras. — Dieser Bücherwurm hört das Gras wachsen.	This bookworm is very conceited.
Er mußte ins Gras beißen.	He had to bite the dust.
Grau. — Lassen Sie sich darüber keine grauen Haaren wachsen.	Do not let this trouble you.
Grauen. — Mir graut vor solchen Gesprächen.	I have a horror of such talk.
Grausen. — Mir grauste. (101)	I was horror-struck.
Greifen. — Das kann man mit den Händen greifen.	That is as clear as day.

Man soll andern nicht in ihre Rechte greifen.	You must not encroach on other people's rights.
Die Räder einer Maschine müssen gut ineinander greifen.	The wheels of an engine must catch well.
Die Krankheit griff schnell um sich.	The illness spread quickly.
Da greifen Sie zu weit!	There you are overstepping bounds!
Greifen Sie nicht zu weit!	Do not indulge in surmises!
Größe. — Malen Sie mich in natürlicher Größe.	Paint me life-size.
Die Zwillinge sind von einer Größe.	The twins are of one size.
Er war ein Schauspieler erster Größe.	He was a first-class actor.
Grün. — Dieser Mensch wird nie auf einen grünen Zweig kommen.	This man will never prosper.
Gründlich. — Ihr müßt das Kapitel gründlich lernen.	You must thoroughly learn the chapter.
Gut. — Ich bin Dir gut.	I wish you well.
Es geht sich gut auf türkischen Teppichen.	It is good walking on Turkey carpets.
Du hast gut reden. (102)	It is easy for you to talk.

Der hat gut schreien; man hört ihn nicht.	It is in vain for him to shout, he will not be heard.
Geht es Ihnen gut?	Are you getting on well?
Er hat zwanzig Pfund bei mir gut.	I owe him £20.
Der hat es gut.	That man has an easy life.
Das wird Ihnen zu gute kommen.	You will be better for it.
Laß es für diesmal gut sein.	It may pass for this time.
Die zehn Pfund wurden ihm gut geschrieben.	The ten pounds were placed to his credit.
Ende gut, alles gut.	All's well that ends well.

H.

Haar.—Bei einem Haare wäre er umgekommen.	He escaped with his life within a hair's breadth.
Er fehlte kein Haar, so wäre er unter dem einfallenden Gemäuer begraben worden.	He was within a hair's breadth of being buried by the falling walls.
Die Frau hat Haare auf den Zähnen.	The woman has plenty of spirit.
Da stehen einem die Haare zu Berge.	That makes one's hair stand on an end.

Haben.—Das haben Sie davon! — That is your thanks!

Es hat nichts auf sich. — It does not signify.

Ich habe nichts dagegen. — I have no objection.

Wen meinen Sie vor sich zu haben? — Whom do you think you have before you?

Sie haben recht, ich habe unrecht. — You are right, I am wrong.

Haften.—Wir haften für ihn. — We answer for him.

Hagestolz.—Der Baron war ein alter Hagestolz. (103) — The baron was an old bachelor.

Hahn.—Der Jäger spannte den Hahn. — The sportsman cocked his gun.

Haken.—Das Ding hat einen Haken. — There is a hitch in this business.

Halber.—Ich that es des Friedens halber. — I did it for the sake of peace.

Halten.—Die Magd hält sich nicht reinlich. — The servant does not keep herself clean.

Sie hält viel auf schöne Kleider. — She is very partial to fine dresses.

Ich halte nicht viel davon. — I do not think much of it.

Paris hielt sich einen ganzen Winter. — Paris held out a whole winter.

Dieser Pächter hält sich schlecht zu Pferde.	This farmer sits his horse badly.
Sie konnte nicht länger an sich halten.	She could not control her temper any longer.

Hand.—Er gab mir die Hand. — He shook hands with me.

Die Bibliothek wurde unter der Hand verkauft.	The library was sold privately.
Er gab mir die Mittel an die Hand.	He put me in the way.
Das Gut kam in andere Hände.	The estate changed hands.
Das hätten Sie nicht aus den Händen lassen sollen.	You ought not to have let that slip.
Die Arbeiter legten Hand ans Werk.	The workmen set to work.
Sehen Sie Ihm auf die Hände!	Watch him!

Handel. — Handel und Gewerbe blühen in unserer Stadt. — Trade and industry are flourishing in our town.

Der Handel im Großen und im Kleinen ist bedeutend.	Commerce, wholesale and retail, is important.
England ist ein handeltreibendes Land.	England is a commercial country.

Er ist Handelsreisender.	He is a commercial traveller.
Sein Vater hat einen Holzhandel.	His father is in the timber trade.
Handeln.—Wovon handelt es sich?	What is it all about?
Händel.—Er fing Händel an.	He picked up a quarrel.
Hang.—Der Knabe hat einen Hang zum Lügen. (104)	The boy is inclined to be untruthful.
Hans bleibt immer Hans.	Jack will never be a gentleman.
Er ist ein Großhans.	He is very consequential.
Der Hanswurst schoß Burzelbäume. (105)	The clown was cutting somersaults.
Hapert.—Es hapert mit der Sache. (106)	There is something wrong about the matter.
Da hapert's!	There is the difficulty!
Harnisch.—Das brachte sie in Harnisch. (107)	That provoked her.
Er geriet in Harnisch.	He got into a passion.
Hase.—Viele Hunde sind des Hasen Tod.	Many hounds are sure to run a hare to ground.
Da sitzt der Hase im Pfeffer! (108)	There is the rub.

Sie ergriffen das Hasenpanier. (109)	They took to their heels.
Hauen.—Das ist weder gehauen noch gestochen.	That has neither rhyme nor reason.
Hauer.—Der Eber hat gewaltige Hauer.	The boar has powerful tusks.
Haufen.—Die feindliche Reiterei wurde über den Haufen geworfen.	The enemy's cavalry were overthrown.
Haupt. — Die Türken wurden aufs Haupt geschlagen.	The Turks were totally defeated.
Er ist jetzt Hauptlehrer an einer Volksschule.	He is now headmaster at a board-school.
Die Hauptleute der Reiterei heißen auf deutsch Rittmeister.	The captains of cavalry are called "Rittmeister" in German
Das Hauptpostamt ist in London.	The General Post Office is in London.
Hauptwörter werden im Deutschen groß geschrieben.	Substantives are written with capital initials in German.
Haus.—Wo sind Sie zu Hause?	Where is your home? or, What is your country?
Ich bin in Deutschland zu Hause.	My native country is Germany.
Der Fremde ist nirgends zu Hause.	The stranger has neither hearth nor home.

E

Es ist kein Mensch zu Hause.	There is no one at home.
Er ist überall zu Hause.	He is well up in everything.
Der Vater war von Hause.	Father was away from home.
Wann gehst Du nach Hause?	When do you go home?
Wir lieben die Hausmannskost.	We like homely fare.
Er hat Hausverstand.	He has common sense.
Heer.—Der Kaiser hielt Heerschau.	The emperor passed the troops in review.
Das Haus steht an der Heerstraße.	The house stands on the highway.
Heilig. — Morgen ist heiliger Abend.	To-morrow is Christmas eve.
Er hatte mir's heilig versprochen.	He had solemnly promised it me.
Heim. — Er hat ein eigenes Heim.	He has his own home.
Sie hatte Heimweh.	She was homesick.
Wann kömmt er heim?	When does he come home?
Heißen. — Die Dienerschaft muß thun, was man sie heißt.	Servants must do what they are told.
Wir hießen die Reisenden willkommen.	We bade the travellers welcome.

Wie heißen Sie?	What is your name?
Ich heiße Leopold. (110)	My name is Leopold.
Der Herr heißt wie ich.	The gentleman has the same name with me.
Es heißt, er sei gefährlich krank.	He is said to be dangerously ill.
Was soll der Lärm heißen?	What is the meaning of this noise?
Wie heißt das auf spanisch?	How do you call that in Spanish?
Das Tuch heißt nichts.	The cloth is no good.
Das will etwas heißen.	That is saying a good deal.
Hier heißt es stramme Arbeit.	Straining every nerve is now the word.
Jetzt heißt es gut treffen!	Now for a good hit!
Helfen. — Alles half nichts.	Nothing would avail.
Hell. — Er schlief bis in den hellen Tag hinein.	He slept till it was broad daylight.
Heller. — Alles war bis auf den letzten Heller verzehrt. (111)	All was spent to the uttermost farthing.
Her. — Komm her, mein Junge. (112)	Come here, my boy!
Die Hand her!	Give me your hand!
Der ist nicht weit her.	He is not of much account.

Herauf.—Kommen Sie zu mir herauf.	Come up to me.
Heraus. — Heraus damit!	Out with it!
Heraus mit der Sprache!	Speak out!
Ich sage Ihnen rund heraus.	I tell you plainly.
Wollen Sie sich heraus bemühen?	Will you give yourself the trouble to come out?
Er nimmt sich viel heraus.	He is very presumptuous.
Herbeilassen (sich). — Er läßt sich nicht dazu herbei.	He will not condescend to do that.
Herein. — Ich rief „herein."	I called out, "Come in."
Herkömmlich.—Das ist hier herkömmlich.	That is the ordinary way here.
Herreise. — Auf meiner Herreise war das Meer sehr stürmisch.	On my voyage here the sea was very rough.
Herumbalgen (sich). — Die Knaben balgten sich herum.	The boys were having a scuffle.
Herumtreiben (sich).— Der Lump treibt sich in Kneipen herum.	The knave is haunting low public houses.

Herumziehen.—Bettler von Profession führen ein herumziehendes Leben. / Professional beggars lead an itinerant life.

Landstreicher ziehen überall herum. / Tramps wander about everywhere.

Heute.—Ich kam heute morgen an. (113) / I arrived this morning.

Heute abend reise ich ab. / I start this evening.

Heute vor acht Tagen starb er. / He died this day week.

Heute vor vierzehn Tagen kamen wir hier an. / We arrived here this day fortnight.

Heute mir, morgen dir. / Everyone in his turn.

Hexe. — Die schmucke kleine Hexe! (113A) / The pretty little rogue of a girl!

Hexerei.—Das ist keine Hexerei. / That is no extraordinary performance.

Hier.—Hier zu Lande trinkt man Thee. / Tea is drunk in this country.

Hierorts. — Hierorts giebt es viele Fabriken. / There are many factories here.

Hin und her. — Ich habe hin und her gedacht. (114) / I have been turning over in my mind.

Das Geld ist hin. / Money is gone.

Hinaus.—Darüber bin ich hinaus. / I do not mind it.

Setzen Sie sich darüber hinaus. — Do not mind that.

Hindurch.—Er studiert das ganze Jahr hindurch. — He is studying all the year round.

Hinein.—Gehen Sie nur hinein. — Just step in.

Es darf niemand zu ihm hinein. — Nobody is allowed to see him.

Hinfahrt.—Auf meiner Hinfahrt hatte ich gute Reisegesellschaft. — On my passage out I had good travelling company.

Hitze.—Man sollte nicht leicht in Hitze geraten. — One ought not easily to fly into a passion.

Hoch.—Der Rhein geht hoch. — The waters of the Rhine are swollen.

Er steht beim Direktor hoch angeschrieben. — He is high in the headmaster's books.

Höchstens.—Sie ist höchstens 16 Jahre alt. — She is sixteen at best.

Hof.—Der Mond hat einen Hof. (115) — There is a halo round the moon.

Hohn.—Er sprach seinen Richtern Hohn. — He bade defiance to his judges.

Holen.—Lassen Sie eine Flasche Wein holen. (116) — Send for a bottle of wine.

Hören.—Er hört nicht gut. — He is rather deaf.
Da hört man nichts. — You cannot hear there.
Der Redner hört sich gerne sprechen. — The orator likes to hear himself.
Ich habe es von Karl gehört. — I have been told by Charles.
Ich hörte bei ihm Philologie. — I attended his lectures on philology.
Der Student hört Kollegien. — The (University) student attends lectures.
Sie ließ sich auf dem Klavier hören. — She performed on the piano.
Das läßt sich hören. — That sounds well.
Lassen Sie bald von sich hören! — Write soon!
Hören Sie nicht auf den Schwätzer! — Do not listen to that babbler!

Hund. — Da liegt der Hund begraben. — There lies the sore point.

Hut. — Seien Sie auf Ihrer Hut! — Be on your guard!

Hütte.—Er ist Hüttenmeister in dem Hüttenwerke. (117) — He is superintendent of the foundries in the smelting works.

I.

Immer.—Es fiel immer mehr Schnee. — More and more snow was falling.
Auf immer und ewig. — For ever and ever.

Das geht immer besser.	That is going better and better.
Wie die Leute nur immer leben können!	How the people can live, I wonder!
Thun Sie es immerhin.	Do it; I do not mind.
In.—Sie lebt in den Tag hinein.	She is living on thoughtlessly.
Sie ist in die sechzig Jahre alt.	She is sixty and odd years old.
Industrieritter. (118)—In dem Gedränge waren viele Industrieritter.	There were many sharpers amongst the crowd.
Inne. — Das hast Du noch nicht inne.	You do not know that quite well yet.
Er hielt plötzlich in seiner Rede inne.	He suddenly stopped in his speech.
Innere (das).—Er ist beim Ministerium des Innern angestellt.	He has an appointment at the Home Office.
Irre. — Da sind Sie irre.	There you are wrong.
Ich wurde an ihm irre.	I did not know what to think of him.
Er redet irre.	He is raving.
Man brachte ihn ins Irrenhaus.	They took him to the insane asylum.
Sie ließ sich irre machen.	She got puzzled.

Irren.—Laſſen Sie ſich das nicht irren. — Do not trouble your head about it.

Sie irren ſich. — You are mistaken.

Irr. — Das war ein Irrgang. — That was a bootless errant.

Dort iſt ein Irrlicht. — There is a Will-with-a-wisp (also Will o'-the-wisp), or Jack-with-a-lantern.

J.

Ja (119)—Ach, da biſt Du ja! — Why, here you are!

Ja, warum nicht gar! — You don't say so!

Thun Sie das ja nicht! — Do not do it on any account!

Kommen Sie ja recht früh! — Mind you come early!

Ich ſagte es ja! — I said so; did I not?

Du ſchickſt es mir; ja? — You will send it to me; won't you?

Sie kennen ihn ja. — I am sure you know him.

Ja, was ich noch bemerken wollte. — By the way, what I was going to add.

Jagen. — Er jagte ſich eine Kugel durch den Kopf. — He blew out his brains.

Ein Huſar jagte durch die Stadt. — A hussar rode at full speed through the town.

Jäger. — Unser Jäger hat einen Hasen geschossen.	Our gamekeeper shot a hare.
Jahr. — Jahr aus Jahr ein.	Year by year.
Sie sind noch in Ihren besten Jahren.	You are still in the prime of life.
Ein Mann von seinen Jahren kennt die Welt.	A man of his age knows the world.
Das giebt sich mit den Jahren.	That will come with the years.
Je. — Je eher desto besser.	The sooner the better.
Kommen Sie; je eher je lieber.	Come; the sooner the better.
Je drei Mann traten ein.	Three men at a time stepped in.
Jedesmalig. — Das kommt auf die jedesmaligen Umstände an.	That depends on the circumstances of the case.
Jetzt. — Thun Sie es jetzt gleich!	Do it this instant!
Jugendstreiche. — Er hat seine Jugendstreiche gemacht.	He has sown his wild oats.
Jung. — Jung gewohnt, alt gethan.	Once a use, and ever a custom.

Jungfernkranz. — Sie hatte einen Jungfernkranz auf dem Kopfe.	She had a bridal wreath on her head.
Jüngst. — Am jüngsten Tage werden wir auferstehen. (120)	We shall rise on the last day.
Das jüngste Gericht ist ein herrliches Gemälde.	The last judgment is a grand picture.
Er ist jüngst angekommen.	He arrived only quite lately.

K.

Kaiserlich. — Wir sind kaiserlich gesinnt. (121)	We side with the Emperor.
Kalt. — Es überlief uns kalt.	We were shivering.
Kanonenstiefel. — Er trug Kanonenstiefel.	He wore jackboots.
Kanzlei. — Der Beamte war auf seiner Kanzlei. (122)	The official was in his office.
Karte. — Wir haben eine Karte von Frankreich gekauft.	We have bought a map of France.
Er sieht ihm in die Karten.	He penetrates his designs.
Das Zigeunerweib schlägt Karten.	The gipsy woman is telling fortunes.

Kauderwelsch. — Die Zigeuner reden Kauderwelsch. (123) — The gipsies are talking gibberish.

Kauen. — Unartige Jungen kauen an den Nägeln. (124) — Ill-behaved boys bite their nails.

Kauf. — Ich gebe Ihnen das in den Kauf. — I give you this into the bargain.

Er reiste mit einem Kauffahrer. — He travelled on board a merchantman.

Kehrt. — Die Compagnie machte kehrt. — The company wheeled round.

Kein. — Kein einziger Käufer meldete sich. — Not a single purchaser turned up.

Es sind keine drei Wochen seit er hier war. — It is not three weeks since he was here.

Das werde ich keineswegs unternehmen. — I shall in no wise undertake that.

Kennen. — Sie sollen mich kennen lernen. (125) — They shall know who I am.

Ich habe ihn kennen lernen. — I have got to know him.

Wo haben Sie ihn kennen lernen? — Where did you get acquainted with him?

Kenner. — Mein Onkel ist ein Kenner von Gemälden. — My uncle is a judge of pictures.

Kenntnis.—Er ist ein Mann von tüchtigen Kenntnissen. — He is a man of sound knowledge.

Kernmensch.—Er ist ein Kernmensch. — He is a man of principle.

Kerzengerade. — Sie hält sich kerzengerade. — She holds herself as straight as a bolt.

Kessel. — Der Dampfkessel sprang. — The boiler exploded.

Kind.—Nennen Sie das Kind bei seinem Namen. — Don't mince matters.

Er verschwand mit Kind und Kegel. — He disappeared with all his family.

Der alte Herr ist ganz zum Kinde geworden. — The old gentleman has grown quite childish.

Das habe ich von Kindesbeinen an gelernt. — I learnt that when yet a child.

Die Kinderzucht ist sehr beschwerlich. — The bringing up of children is very troublesome.

Kirschwasser. — Das Kirschwasser wird aus den Kirschkernen destilliert. — Cherry brandy is distilled from the kernels of cherries.

Klang.—Der Name hat hier einen guten Klang. — The name has a good ring here.

Er wurde mit Sang und Klang empfangen. — He was received with music and ringing of bells.

Klappen.—Hören Sie einmal; das klappt ja nicht! — Look here; that won't do!

Klar.—Ich bin noch nicht ganz im klaren. — I do not quite see my way as yet.

Endlich bin ich mit ihr ins klare gekommen. — At last I got to a clear understanding with her.

Klatsch.—Er ist ein Müßiggänger und darum ein Klatschbruder. — He is an idler, and therefore a gossip.

Klatscherei.—Das ist eine gemeine Klatscherei. — That is low gossip.

Klein.—Geben Sie mir ein klein wenig. — Give me very little (a "wee bit").

Er ist ein Kleingeist. — He is narrow-minded.

Sei nicht kleinmütig. — Do not be despondent.

Haben Sie Kleingeld? — Have you any change?

Kleinigkeit.—Das ist ihm eine Kleinigkeit. — That is child's play for him.

Er erzürnt sich wegen einer Kleinigkeit. — He gets angry for nothing.

Er ist ein Kleinigkeitskrämer. — He makes a great fuss about nothing.

Klinge.—Die Rebellen mußten über die Klinge springen.
The rebels were put to the sword.

Klingen.—Er bezahlte in klingender Münze.
He paid in ready money.

Das Heer zog mit klingendem Spiel in die Stadt ein.
The army made their entry into the town with drums beating and bands playing.

Klug.—Sie sind nicht klug!
You don't mean to say so!

Der Arme ist nicht recht klug!
Poor man, he is not right in his mind.

Daraus kann ich nicht klug werden.
I can make neither head nor tail of it.

Kniff.—Ich kenne seine Kniffe.
I know his dodges.

Kollegium.—Die Professoren lesen und die Studenten hören Kollegien.
The professors *give* and the students *attend* lectures.

Kommen.—Da kömmt ein Mann in aller Hast gelaufen.
There comes a man running in all haste.

Ich lasse meine Bücher von London kommen.
I send to London for my books.

Er ist nie unter die Leute gekommen.
He has never been in society.

Ich bin an den Unrechten gekommen.	I applied to the wrong man.
Wie kömmst du auf den Gedanken?	What makes you think so?
Damit dürfen Sie ihr nicht kommen.	She will not listen to that.
Sie kommen nicht mit einander aus.	They do not get along together.
Er wird nie zu etwas kommen.	He will never come to anything.
So müssen Sie mir nicht kommen.	You must not speak so rudely to me.
Jetzt kömmt es an dich.	Now is your turn.
Es mag kommen, was will.	Come what may.
Es kam zu Schlägen.	They came to blows.
Wie kömmt das?	How is that?
Können.—Ich hätte es thun können.	I might have done it.
Ich kann nicht umhin zu sagen.	I cannot help saying.
Sie sehen ja, er kann nicht mehr.	I am sure you see he is quite exhausted.
Das kann sein.	That may be.
Ich kann ihn wohl irgendwo gesehen haben.	It is quite likely I may have seen him somewhere.
Kann ich jetzt gehen?	May I go now?

Das kann er nicht. — He cannot do that.

Kopf.—Wir steckten unsere Köpfe zusammen. — We laid our heads together.

Er singt mit einer Kopfstimme. — He sings falsetto.

Korb. — Sie gab ihm einen Korb. (126) — She refused him.

Er hat einen Korb bekommen. — He was refused.

Kost.—Er geht dort in die Kost. — He is a boarder there.

Ich habe meine Tochter bei ihrer Lehrerin in die Kost gegeben. — I put my daughter to board with her teacher.

Kosten.—Dieser Teppich kostet mich vier Pfund. — I paid £4 for this carpet.

Sie ließ es sich etwas kosten. — She went to great expense.

Ich muß gehen, koste es, was es wolle. — I must go at any cost.

Krank.—Er wurde gefährlich krank. — He fell dangerously ill.

Kränzchen.—Die Damen haben ein Kränzchen. — The ladies have a little club of their own.

Kraus. — Die Jungen treiben es zu kraus. — The boys are going too far in their unruliness.

Krebs.—Du gehst den Krebsgang. — You are going backward.

Krumm.—Er sah mich krumm an. — He was scowling at me.

Die Sträflinge wurden krumm geschlossen. — The convicts were chained down in a crooked position.

Küche.—Es giebt heute nur kalte Küche. — We have only cold meat to-day.

Kuckuck. — Das ist ja zum Kuckuck holen. (127) — That is too bad.

Kuh.—Die Kinder spielten blinde Kuh. — The children were playing blindman's buff.

Kümmern.—Was kümmert mich das? — What is that to me?

Ich kümmere mich nicht darum. — I do not trouble my head about it.

Kürzer.—Er mußte den Kürzern ziehen. — He got the worst of it.

Sie kam zu kurz. — She came off a loser.

L.

Lachen.—Was giebt es da zu lachen? — Why do you laugh there?

Das Herz lachte mir im Leibe. — My heart leaped for joy.

Laden. — Der Matrose hat schief geladen. — The sailor is half-seas over.

Der Arme hat sich vielen Kummer auf den Hals geladen. — The poor fellow has brought much trouble upon himself.

Die Laden der Läden waren geschlossen.	The shutters of the shops were shut.
Laken.—Die Laken sind nicht rein	The sheets are not clean.
Land. — Ich habe zu Wasser und zu Lande gereist.	I have travelled by land and by water.
Das Boot stieß vom Lande.	The boat left the shore.
Wir fuhren am Lande hin.	We were hugging the coast.
Mein Vater lebt auf dem Lande.	My father lives in the country.
Bei uns zu Lande trinkt man Wein.	In my country they drink wine.
Der Fürst hat sich außer Landes begeben.	The prince has gone abroad.
Das sind Landesverwiesene.	These are exiles.
Lang. — Mir wird die Zeit lang.	Time hangs heavy on me.
Er raucht den ganzen Tag lang.	He smokes all day long.
Langen.—Er langte in die Tasche.	He made a dive into his pocket.
Längstens.—Ich komme längstens nächsten Monat.	I shall come next month at the latest.

Lärm.—Viel Lärm um nichts. — Much ado about nothing.

Lassen.—Wo haben Sie Ihren Kopf gelassen? — Where did you leave your wits?

Laß das! — Leave that alone!

Er läßt sich leicht betrügen. — He is easily taken in.

Lassen Sie sich raten. — Let me advise you.

Man muß ihr das lassen — There you must do her justice.

Sie sollten die Bücher binden lassen. (128) — You ought to get the books bound.

Napoleon ließ ihn erschießen. — Napoleon had him shot.

Er ließ den Arzt rufen. — He sent for the doctor.

Der Rock läßt Ihnen schön. — The coat suits you well.

Es läßt gelehrt, wenn man eine Brille trägt. — You look learned when you wear spectacles.

Last.—Ich wollte meinen Eltern nicht zur Last fallen. — I did not wish to hang upon my parents' hands.

Lateiner.—Er ist ein guter Lateiner. — He is a good Latinist.

Laufen lassen.—Der Schutzmann ließ den Dieb laufen. — The policeman let the thief escape.

Laune.—Sie sind heute nicht bei guter Laune. — You are not in high spirits to-day.

Launisch.—Sie ist sehr launisch.	She is very peevish.
Lehre.—Er ist bei einem Buchbinder in der Lehre.	He is apprenticed to a bookbinder.
Laß dir das zur Lehre dienen.	Let that be a lesson to you.
Lehrer.—In unserer Stadt ist ein Lehrerseminar.	There is a Normal College in our town.
Leichdorn.—Leichdörner heißen auf deutsch auch Hühneraugen. (129)	Corns are also called "fowls' eyes" (in German).
Leiche.—Meine Brüder sind zur Leiche eines Nachbars gegangen.	My brothers went to a neighbour's funeral.
Der Leichenwagen wurde von zwei Rappen (see that word) gezogen.	The hearse was drawn by two black horses.
Leid.—Die Damen tragen Leid.	The ladies are in mourning.
Sie that es mir zuleide.	She did it to vex me.
Er sagte, er wolle sich ein Leids anthun.	He said he would do away with himself.
Zu unserem großen Leidwesen ist das Buch nicht zu finden.	To our great regret the book cannot be found.
Leid.—Es thut mir herzlich leid.	I am heartily sorry.

Es that uns sehr leid um die gute Frau. — We were very sorry for the good woman.

Leiden.—Ich kann Ehrabschneider nicht leiden. — I cannot bear backbiters.

Leide und meide. — Bear and forbear.

Er ist in unserem Verein gern gelitten. — He is popular in our club.

Leider.—Ich war leider nicht zu Hause. — To my regret I was not at home.

Leider ist das nicht so. — I am sorry to say that is not so.

Leidig. — Das leidige Zahnweh läßt mich nicht schlafen. — That nasty toothache will not let me sleep.

Leier.—Er kömmt immer mit der alten Leier. — He is always treating us to the same old story.

Lenken. —Der Mensch denkt, Gott lenkt. — Man proposes, God disposes.

Lernen.—Das Kind hat gehen lernen. (130) — The child has learnt to walk.

Er ist ein gelernter Dreher. (131) — He is a turner by trade.

Lesen. — Sie hat sehr viel gelesen. — She is very well-read.

Der Herr Professor liest heute nicht. — The professor does not lecture to-day.

Heute wird nicht gelesen. — There is no lecture to-day.

Das Buch läßt sich lesen.	It is a readable book.
Leuchten.—Das leuchtet jedermann in die Augen.	That is evident to everybody.
Leute.— Er kennt seine Leute.	He knows whom he has to deal with.
Der König verlor Land und Leute.	The king lost his throne.
Licht.— Goethe hat zu Frankfurt das Licht der Welt erblickt.	Goethe was born at Frankfort.
Lieb.—Wenn es dir lieb ist, so gehen wir spazieren. (132)	If you like, we will take a walk.
Wenn dir dein Leben lieb ist, so schweige.	If you value your life, be silent.
Ich weiß nur Liebes und Gutes von ihr.	I can only speak most highly of her.
Lieber.—Ich gehe lieber.	I prefer to go.
Es wäre mir lieber, er käme nicht.	I should rather wish he would not come.
Liefern. — Hier wurde eine Schlacht geliefert.	Here a battle was fought.
Der Gärtner liefert uns Gemüse.	The gardener supplies us with vegetables.
Liegen. — Die Köchin ließ alles stehen und liegen.	The cook left everything in the wildest disorder.

Die Deutschen lagen vor Paris.	The Germans were lying encamped before Paris.
Es liegt mir nichts daran.	It is of no consequence to me.
Es lag nicht an mir.	It was not my fault.
Was liegt daran?	What does it matter?
Wenn es nur daran liegt.	If that is all.
Daran liegt es eben.	That is just it.
Lohnen. — Die Sache lohnt sich der Mühe nicht.	It is not worth while.
Los. — Was ist denn da los?	Why, what is the matter there?
Nur frisch darauf los, meine Jungen!	Go at it, boys, with a will!
Das sind lose Gesellen.	They are good-for-nothing fellows.
Warte nur, du kleiner loser Schelm!	Look out, you little rogue!
Lösen. — Die Obsthändlerin hat heute noch nichts gelöst. (133)	The woman at the fruit-stall has not yet taken any money to-day.
Geben Sie ihr etwas zu lösen.	Buy something of her.
Haben Sie Ihr Billet gelöst?	Have you taken your ticket?

Lofungswort. — Was war das Losungswort?   What was the watchword?

Luft. — Haben Sie Lust eine Spazierfahrt zu machen?   Do you feel inclined to take a drive?

Der will ich die Lust zum Klatschen benehmen.   I will sicken her of her gossiping.

M.

Machen. — Wieviel machen dreimal vierzehn?   How many are three times fourteen?

Das macht nichts.   That does not matter.

Ich lasse mir einen Anzug machen.   I am getting a new suit made for myself.

Daraus mache ich mir nichts.   I do not mind that.

Machen Sie sich keine Mühe.   Do not take the trouble.

Machen Sie es kurz!   Be quick!

Er macht sich groß.   He is boasting.

Womit macht er sich groß?   What is he boasting of?

Er hat all seine Habe zu Gelde gemacht.   He turned all his belongings into ready money.

Sie machen sich nutzlose Sorgen.   You are at pains to no purpose.

Das wird sich machen.   There is a chance for it.

Er hat sich gut gemacht. — He came out well.

Das Kind macht sich gut in dem Jäckchen. — The child looks well in that jacket.

Er macht sich überall beliebt. — He earns golden opinions everywhere.

Der Spitzbube machte sich aus dem Staube. — The rogue ran away.

Machwerk. — Das ist ein elendes Machwerk. — That is wretched bungling.

Maiblümchen. — Wir fanden dort viele Maiblümchen. — We found many lilies of the valley there.

Maikäfer. — Die Maikäfer sind schädliche Insekten. — Cockchafers are hurtful insects.

Man. — Man weiß das wohl. — That is well known.

Man glaube es oder nicht. — Whether they believe it or not.

Mangeln. — Es mangelt mir an Büchern. — I want books.

Sie läßt es sich an nichts mangeln. — She does not deny herself anything.

Mann. — Er kann seine Ware nicht an den Mann bringen. — He cannot dispose of his goods; also— This knowledge is of no use to him.

Das Schiff ging mit Mann und Maus unter. — The ship went down with crew and cargo.

Sie standen fünf Mann hoch.	They stood five deep.
Ihr Mann war nicht zu Hause.	Her husband was **not** at home.
Ein Mann ein Wort.	An honest man is **as** good as his word.
Das Heer zählt hunderttausend Mann zu Fuß.	The army amounts **to** 100,000 foot.
Er hat einen Mann gestellt.	He has furnished a substitute.
Sie ist ein Mannweib.	She is a virago.
Mantel.—Er hängt den Mantel nach dem Winde.	He is complying with the times.
Maß.—Sie halten weder Maß noch Ziel.	They exceed all bounds.
Halten Sie stets Maß.	Always keep within bounds.
Maul.—Man hatte den Hunden Maulkörbe umgehängt.	They had muzzled the dogs.
Der Knabe hatte eine Maultrommel.	The boy had a Jew's harp.
Er hat Maulaffen feil.	He is staring vacantly.
Er gab ihm eine Maulschelle.	He slapped his face.
Maus.—Wenn die Katze nicht zu Hause ist, tanzen die Mäuse.	When the cat is away, the mice will play.

Mehr. — Kein Wort mehr!	Not another word!
Das ist nicht mehr als billig.	That is but fair.
Meinen.—Ich meine es gut mit dir.	I am your well-wisher.
Sie meint es nicht böse.	She means no harm.
Meinung.— Dem will ich meine Meinung sagen.	I will give him a piece of my mind.
Meister.—Er hat in ihm seinen Meister gefunden.	He has met with his match in him.
Übung macht den Meister.	Practice makes perfect.
Melden. — Ich melde hiemit den Empfang Ihres Briefes.	I herewith acknowledge the receipt of your letter.
Mein Bruder hat sich zu der Stelle gemeldet.	My brother applied for the post.
Menge.—Er hat Gold die Menge.	He has plenty of money.
Menschlich.— Irren ist menschlich.	Anyone is liable to make mistakes.
Sollte mir etwas Menschliches begegnen.	Should I happen to die.
Merken.—Merken Sie sich das!	Remember that!

Minder.— Er ist minderjährig. — He is a minor.

Das Kind merkt auf alles. — The child is taking notice of everything.

Mit.— Ich schicke die Bücher mit der Post. — I am sending the books by post.

Mit dem Glockenschlage trat er ein. — He stepped in upon the stroke of the clock.

Kommen Sie mit? — Are you coming along?

Wollen Sie mithalten? — Will you join us in our meal?

Spielen Sie mit? — Will you join us in our game?

Man kann nicht alles mitmachen. — One cannot join in everything.

Mögen.— Er möchte wohl, wenn er könnte. — He would if he could.

Ich möchte gerne ausgehen. — I should like to go out.

„Ich mag nicht" ist nicht höflich. — I won't is not polite.

Möglichstes. — Thun Sie Ihr möglichstes. — Do your utmost.

Morgen.— Morgen früh reisen wir ab. — We start to-morrow morning.

Morgen abend kommt er. — He comes to-morrow evening.

Morgens arbeite ich. — I work in the morning.

Mühe. — Er ließ sich keine Mühe verdrießen.	He spared no pains.
Ich habe die Mühe umsonst gehabt.	My labour was in vain.
Es lohnt sich nicht der Mühe.	It is not worth while.
Mund. — Er weiß reinen Mund zu halten.	He knows how to keep his counsel.
Sie nehmen mir das Wort aus dem Munde.	That is just what I was going to say.
Sie hat den Mund auf dem rechten Flecke.	She has a sharp tongue.
Spitze den Mund nicht so!	Do not screw up your mouth so!
Münze. — Ich habe ihn in barer Münze bezahlt.	I gave him a Roland for an Oliver.
Münzen. — Das war auf mich gemünzt.	I was meant by that.
Musik. — Sie machen Musik.	They are performing.
Das Stück wurde in Musik gesetzt.	The piece was set to music.
Müssen. — Es müßte denn sein, daß er krank wäre.	Unless he be ill.
Mut. — Mir ist nicht wohl zu Mute. (134)	I feel uncomfortable.

Seien Sie gutes Mutes!	Cheer up!
Mir war sonderbar zu Mute.	I felt queer.
Sie müssen ihr Mut machen.	You must encourage her.

N.

Nach.—Kehren Sie sich nach Süden.	Turn to the south.
Wir gingen nach den Bergen zu.	We went in the direction of the hills.
Es ist ein viertel auf acht nach meiner Uhr.	It is a quarter past seven by my watch.
Dem Scheine nach ist er sehr stark.	Apparently he is very strong.
Wir zeichnen nach der Natur.	We draw from nature.
Nach Christi Geburt.	Anno Domini.
Nächst.—Bei der nächsten Gelegenheit werde ich schreiben.	I shall write on the first opportunity.
Man soll seinem Nächsten in der Not beistehen. (135)	One must help one's neighbour in his need.
Jeder ist sich selbst der Nächste.	Charity begins at home.
Nacht. — Guter Rat kommt über Nacht.	Sleep over it.

Er ist bei Nacht und Nebel durchgegangen. — He escaped by night.

Nähe. — Ich habe mir das Haus in der Nähe betrachtet. — I looked at the house more closely.

Name. — Er ist unter dem Namen nicht bekannt. — He is not known by that name.

Ein Schauspieler, Bauer mit Namen. — An actor called Bauer.

Das ist nicht sein Namenszug. — That is not his signature.

Narren. — Jedem Narren gefällt seine Kappe. — Everyone thinks his own hobby the best.

Nase. — Er hat eine Nase bekommen. — He was reprimanded.

Unser Garten stach ihr gewaltig in die Nase. — She envied us our garden.

Natur. — Das ist ein sonderbares Naturereignis. — That is a strange phenomenon.

Wir haben hier ein ausgezeichnetes Naturalienkabinett. — We have here an excellent museum of natural history.

Natürlich. — Natürlicherweise. — Of course.

Nebel. — Die Nebelbilder waren reizend. — The dissolving views were charming.

Neben. — Neben andern Dingen erwähnte er auch dieses. — Among other things he also mentioned this.

Nehmen. — Er läßt sich das nicht nehmen. — He will not be dissuaded from it.

Das kann ich nicht auf mich nehmen. — I cannot undertake that.

Er nahm es falsch. — He misunderstood it.

Es nimmt mich Wunder. — I wonder.

Da sollten Sie keinen Anstand nehmen. — You ought not to hesitate.

Mein Freund hat soeben Abschied von uns genommen. — My friend has just taken leave of us.

Neu. — Das Brot ist neubacken. — The bread is new.

Das ist etwas ganz Neubackenes. — That is something quite new-fangled.

Der Löffel war aus Neusilber. — The spoon was German silver.

Nicht. — Nicht doch! — Certainly not.

Sie sind ein Deutscher, nicht wahr? — You are German, are you not?

Mit nichten. — By no means.

Er ist lange nicht so reich wie Sie glauben. — He is not nearly so rich as you think.

Er machte alle ihre Anschläge zu nichte. — He baffled all their plans.

G

Nichts. — Er weiß so viel wie nichts. He knows next to nothing.
Wenn es weiter nichts ist. If that is all.
Das hat nichts zu bedeuten. That does not signify.
Daraus wird nichts. Nothing will come of it.
Nichts dergleichen. Nothing of the kind.
Noch. — Geben Sie mir noch eine Tasse. Give me another cup.
Noch einmal. Once more.
Er kann noch dreißig Jahre leben. He may live 30 years longer.
Er bleibt noch so lange. He stays ever so long.
Nur. — Fahren Sie nur weiter. Just go on.
Thun Sie es nur auch. Only be sure to do it.
Wenn er nur nicht ausgegangen ist. I only hope he will not be out.
Nuß. — Er hat mir eine harte Nuß aufzubeißen gegeben. He set me a hard task.

O.

Oben. — Deine Schwester ist oben. Your sister is upstairs.
Oberst. — Der Oberst heißt Oberst, weil er die oberste Gewalt im Regimente hat. The colonel has his German name „Oberst," from his having supreme power in the regiment.

Die Äpfel lagen zuoberst. — The apples were lying uppermost.

Oder. — Gehen Sie schnell, oder Sie kommen zu spät. — Go quickly, or else you will be late.

Ohne. — Das ist nicht ohne. — There is some truth in it.

Ohnmacht. — Sie fiel in Ohnmacht. (136) — She fainted.

Ohr. — Er war ganz Ohr. — He was all attention.

Er ist bis über die Ohren in Schulden. — He is in debts over head and ears.

Ort. — Die Kohlen werden an Ort und Stelle abgeliefert. — Coal is delivered on the premises.

Das werde ich gehörigen Ortes anbringen. — I shall bring this to the notice of the proper authority.

Ich habe ein gutes Ortsgedächtnis. — I have a good local memory.

Ostern. — Sie haben Ostern gehalten. (137) — They received the Sacrament at Easter.

P.

Paar. — Kommen Sie in ein paar Tagen. — Come in a day or two.

Die Feinde wurden zu Paaren getrieben. — The enemy were routed.

Pacht.—Ich habe das Gut in Pacht. — I have the lease of the estate.

Er hat Haus und Garten in Pacht genommen. — He has taken the lease of the house and garden.

Wieviel Pachtgeld bezahlt dieser Pächter? — What rent does this tenant farmer pay?

Pantoffel. — Er stand unter dem Pantoffel. (138) — He was henpecked.

Partie.—Sind Sie bei der Partie? — Will you be one of the party?

Man veranstaltete eine Partie. — An excursion was arranged.

Wir machten eine Partie Whist. — We had a game of whist.

Passen. — Das paßt nicht dazu. — That will not match it.

Das paßt für solche Leute. — That will do for such people.

Das paßt sich nicht für ein Mädchen. — That is not becoming for a girl.

Patron. — Er ist ein lustiger Patron. — He is a jolly fellow.

Person.—Er war groß von Person. — He was of tall stature.

Pferd.—Sie haben die Pferde hinter den Wagen gespannt. — You have put the cart before the horse.

Das ist mein Steckenpferd.	That is my hobby.
Pflegen. — Sie pflegt ihren alten Vater.	She is nursing her old father.
Wir pflegten Rats mit einander.	We took counsel together.
Sie müssen sich pflegen.	You must take care of yourself.
Mein Vater pflegte zu sagen.	My father used to say.
Es geschah eben, wie es gewöhnlich zu geschehen pflegt.	Why, it happened as things generally will happen.
Pfleger. — Der Notar ist der Pfleger dieser Kinder.	The attorney is the guardian of these children.
Plan. — Der Baumeister macht den Plan.	The architect is drawing the plan.
Er hat allerlei Pläne im Kopfe.	He has all sorts of schemes in his head.
Platz. — Platz gemacht!	Clear the way!
Sie nehmen zu viel Platz ein.	You are taking too much room.
Stellen Sie das Buch wieder an seinen Platz.	Put the book back to its place.
Post. — Der Brief kam mit der heutigen Post.	The letter came by to-day's post.
Schreiben Sie gefälligst mit umgehender Post.	Please write by return.

Ich gehe jetzt auf die Post.	I am now going to post.
Ich versende das Paket mit der Post.	I am sending the parcel by post.
Pracht.—Das ist eine wahre Pracht!	That is really splendid!
Prämie. — Karl hat sechs Prämien bekommen.	Charles took 6 prizes.
Preis.—Das thue ich um keinen Preis.	I won't do that for all the world.
Die Stadt wurde preisgegeben.	The town was given up to pillage.
Prellen. — Sie müssen sich nicht prellen lassen.	You must not allow yourself to be overreached.
Probe.—Ich nehme Sie auf Probe.	I take you on trial.
Er hat die Probe bestanden.	He stood the test.
Ich zeigte ihm eine Probe.	I was showing him a sample.
Prozeß.—Es wurde ihm wegen Betrügerei der Prozeß gemacht.	He was brought to trial for cheating.
Er fing einen Prozeß mit uns an.	He instituted legal proceedings against us.
Pulver.—Er hat noch kein Pulver gerochen.	He has never seen service.

Er hat das Pulver nicht erfunden.	He won't set the Thames on fire.
Der Mensch ist keinen Schuß Pulver wert.	The fellow is not worth powder and shot.
Punkt. — Hier macht man einen Punkt.	Here you put a full stop.
Er kam Punkt zwölf Uhr.	He came at 12 o'clock precisely.
Ich stand auf dem Punkte, zu schreiben.	I was about to write.

Q.

Quer.—Quer gegenüber wohnt der Bürgermeister.	The mayor lives over the way.
Wir liefen querfeldein.	We ran across the fields.
Er ist querköpfig.	He is wrong-headed.
Quere.—Der Geometer maß des Feld in die Länge und in die Quere (139.)	The surveyor measured the field in its length and breadth.
Komme mir nicht mehr in die Quere.	Do not cross my path any more.
Quittung.—Ich werde Ihnen eine Quittung ausstellen.	I shall write a receipt for you.

R.

Rad. — Er ist das fünfte Rad am Wagen.	He is of no use whatever.

Der Kapitän stand auf dem Radkasten.	The captain stood on the paddle-box.
Rappe.—Er fährt mit zwei Rappen (140.)	He drives two black horses.
Sie ritten auf des Schusters Rappen.	They trudged on foot.
Rat.—Da war guter Rat teuer (141.)	That was a difficult question.
Dazu kann Rat werden.	That may be remedied.
Ich wußte mir keinen Rat.	I was at my wit's end.
Wir gingen mit ihm zu Rate.	We deliberated with him.
Die Ratsherren sind auf dem Rathause.	The councillors are at the town hall.
Raten.—Lassen Sie sich raten!	Be advised!
Rechnung.—Er machte uns einen Strich durch die Rechnung.	He thwarted our plans.
Meine Tochter führt die Rechnung.	My daughter keeps the accounts.
Recht.—Mir ist alles recht.	I agree to everything.
Wenn es Ihnen recht ist, so können wir jetzt gehen.	We can go now, if you like.
Der ist mir auch der Rechte!	He is a nice fellow indeed! (*ironically*).

Das ist recht und billig.	That is fair and reasonable.
Da bist du an den Rechten gekommen.	There you have found your match.
Da geht es nicht mit rechten Dingen zu (142.)	I smell a rat in this business; also, there is witchcraft in this.
Ich thue es recht gern.	I am quite pleased to do it.
Rechts.—Rechts um!	Right face!
Rede.—Wovon ist die Rede?	What is the matter in hand?
Was ist der langen Rede kurzer Sinn?	What is the meaning of that rigmarole?
Davon kann keine Rede sein.	That is out of the question.
Achten Sie auf meine Rede.	Mind my words.
Vergessen Sie Ihre Rede nicht.	Do not forget what you were going to say.
Ich stellte ihn wegen seiner Lüge zu Rede.	I took him to task for his falsehood.
Reden wir von etwas anderm.	Let us change the subject.
Reden.—Er wird schon mit sich reden lassen.	He will listen to reason.
Reden ist Silber, Schweigen ist Gold.	Least said soonest mended.

Machen Sie nicht so viel Redens davon.	Do not make such a fuss about it.
Rege. — Das machte ihre Eifersucht rege.	That roused her jealousy.
Regen. — Wir sind aus dem Regen in die Traufe gekommen. (143.)	We have jumped from the frying-pan into the fire.
Register. — Er steht im schwarzen Register.	He is down in the black book.
Wie viele Register hat die Orgel?	How many stops has the organ?
Reich. — Der Kaiser ist das Oberhaupt des Reiches.	The Emperor is the head of the Empire.
Elsaß und Lothringen heißen Reichslande.	Alsace and Lorraine are called Imperial Territories.
Reichen. — Er reicht ihm das Wasser nicht.	He is not fit to hold a candle to him.
Reihe. — Jetzt kömmt die Reihe an mich.	Now it is my turn.
Sie standen in Reihe und Glied.	They stood in rank and file.
Der General stellte seine Truppen in Reihe und Glied.	The general drew up his troops.

Rein. — Ich will mit Ihnen ins Reine kommen.
I will come to an understanding with you.

Das ist rein unmöglich.
That is quite impossible.

Reise. — Sie hat sich auf Reisen begeben.
She has gone abroad.

Reißen. — Wenn alle Stricke reißen, dann wandere ich aus.
If the worst come to the worst, I shall emigrate.

Er hat das Gliederreißen.
He has the rheumatism.

Reiten. — Hier liegt reitende Artillerie.
There is some horse-artillery stationed here.

Richten. — Sie müssen sich nicht nach uns richten.
You must not follow our example.

Das Trinken hat ihn zu Grunde gerichtet.
Drinking has ruined him.

Richtigkeit. — Damit hat es seine Richtigkeit.
That is quite correct.

Rind. — Ochsen, Stiere, Kühe und Kälber heißen auf deutsch Rinder.
Oxen, bulls, cows, and calves are called "Rinder" in German.

Rotbraun. — Der Rotbraune ist lahm.
The bay horse is lame.

Ruf. — Der Professor hat einen Ruf nach Leipzig erhalten.
The professor has been called to fill a chair at Leipzig University.

Er steht in gutem Rufe.	He has a good name.
Verleumder bringen ihre Nebenmenschen in übeln Ruf.	Backbiters take away their fellow creatures' characters.
Ruhe.—Der alte Direktor hat sich zur Ruhe begeben.	The old headmaster has retired.
Der Beamte ist in den Ruhestand versetzt worden.	The official has been pensioned off.
Ruhig.—Ruhig dort!	Be quiet there!
Seien Sie nur ruhig.	Never fear.
Rühren.—Rührt euch!	Be quick!
Rührt euch nicht, ihr Jungen!	Do not move, boys!
Rümpfen.—Sie rümpfte die Nase darüber.	She turned up her nose at it.
Runde.—Die Wache macht die Runde.	The watch are going their round.
Die Karte umfaßt dreißig Meilen in die Runde.	The map comprises 30 miles round.
Rüsten.—Die Feinde rüsten.	The enemies are making preparations.

S.

Sache.—Bleiben Sie bei der Sache.	Stick to the point.
Das gehört nicht zur Sache.	That has nothing to do with the subject in hand.

Das ist seine Sache.	That is his look-out.
Tadeln ist meine Sache nicht.	I am not fond of fault-finding.
Nehmen Sie Ihre sieben Sachen.	Take your things.
Sagen.—Was Sie nicht sagen?	You do not say so?
Unter uns gesagt ist es einerlei.	Between you and me, it is all the same.
Was wollen Sie damit sagen?	What do you mean by that?
Das sagen Sie nur so.	You are pleased to say that.
Ich habe mir sagen lassen.	I have been told.
Was will das sagen?	What is the meaning of that?
Der hat vom Glück zu sagen, daß er nicht mit dem Zuge reiste.	It was lucky for him not to have travelled by that train.
Ich sage Ihnen Dank.	I give you thanks.
Sammeln.—Ich muß mich erst sammeln.	I must first collect my thoughts.
Sattel.—Er sitzt fest im Sattel.	He sits his horse well.
Ich ziehe das Sattelstück vor.	I prefer the saddle (meat).
Schade.—Das verkaufen wir mit Schaden. (144.)	We are selling that below price.

Es ist ewig schade. Es ist jammerschade.	It is a thousand pities.
Schadet.—Was schadet es?	What harm can it do?
Es schadet nichts.	It does not signify.
Seine Unbedachtsamkeit schadet ihm.	His inconsiderateness is against him.
Schadlos.—Er hat sich schadlos gehalten.	He indemnified himself.
Schaffen.—Damit will ich nichts zu schaffen haben.	I will have nothing to do with it.
Sie machte mir viel zu schaffen.	She gave me a deal of trouble.
Du machst dir zuviel zu schaffen.	You meddle with too many things.
Schaffner.—Rufen Sie den Schaffner.	Call the *(railway)* guard.
Schalk. — Er ist ein Schalk (145.)	He is a wag.
Scharf. — Die Knaben werden in jener Schule scharf gehalten.	The boys at that school are under strict discipline.
Schatten.—Das Ding hat seine Schattenseiten.	The matter has its disadvantages.
Schau.—Man muß die Tugend nicht zur Schau tragen.	One must not make a display of virtue.

Schein.—Er las beim Scheine einer Lampe.
He was reading by the light of a lamp.

Der Schein trügt.
Appearances are deceitful.

Es war nur ein Scheingefecht.
It was only a sham fight.

Die Pharisäer waren Scheinheilige.
The Pharisees were hypocrites.

Sie war scheintot.
She was in a trance.

Haben Sie Ihren Impfschein?
Have you got your certificate of vaccination?

Ja, und auch meinen Geburtsschein.
Yes, and also my certificate of birth.

Scheiterhaufen.—Huß starb auf dem Scheiterhaufen (146.)
Huss died at the stake.

Schellen.—Es hat geschellt.
There was a bell.

Schelten.—Er schalt ihn einen Bengel (147.)
He called him a rude fellow.

Schenken.—Es soll dir geschenkt sein.
I will forgive you.

Ich habe das geschenkt bekommen.
I got that as a present.

Die Königin schenkte ihm das Leben.
The queen pardoned him.

Scherz.—Er macht gern Scherze. — He likes to crack jokes.

Mit alten Leuten muß man nicht Scherz treiben. — You must not make sport of old people.

Scherzen. — Er läßt nicht mit sich scherzen. — He will not be trifled with.

Scheu. — Unsere Pferde wurden scheu. — Our horses shied.

Schicken (sich).—Sie kann sich nicht darein schicken. — She cannot get accustomed to it.

Das schickt sich nicht für dich. — That is unbecoming for you.

Schießen.— Die Rekruten schießen blind. — The recruits are firing blank cartridges.

Die Soldaten schossen scharf. — The soldiers were firing ball cartridges.

Das Dorf wurde in Grund und Boden geschossen. — The village was battered down by the fire from the guns.

Du hast fehlgeschossen. — You missed.

Die Schüler schießen viele Böcke. — Schoolboys make many mistakes.

Schild. — Die Schildwache steht im Schilderhäuschen. (148) — The sentry is standing in the sentry box.

Schimmel. — Der Schimmel steht im Stall. (149) — The white horse is in the stable.

Schimmelig. — Das Brot war schimmelig.　The bread was mouldy.

Schlafen. — Wünsche wohl zu schlafen!　Good night!

Gehen Sie schlafen?　Are you going to bed?

Schläfchen. — Er macht ein Schläfchen.　He is taking a nap.

Schlag. — Der Feind ergab sich ohne einen Schlag zu thun.　The enemy surrendered without striking a blow.

Der Junge bekam Schläge.　The youngster got a thrashing.

Der Mann ist von gutem Schlage.　He is a "good sort."

Schlagen. — Die Zinsen werden zum Kapital geschlagen.　The interests are added to the capital.

Die ganze Partei schlug sich zu ihm.　The whole party went over to him.

Schlagen Sie sich das aus den Gedanken.　Put this out of your thoughts.

Schlecht. — Handle schlecht und recht. (150)　Be honest and upright.

Schleicher. — Ich bin kein Freund von Schleichern und Schleichwegen.　I am no friend of sneaks and underhand ways.

Schleichhändler sind Schmuggler.　„Schleichhändler" are smugglers.

Schließen.—Der Kapitän ließ ihn in Ketten schließen. — The captain had him put in irons.

Was schließen Sie daraus? — What do you infer from that?

Es ist eine geschlossene Gesellschaft. — It is a club.

Schlimm. — Er ist schlimm daran. — He is in a bad plight.

Schmal.—Bei den Leuten geht es schmal her. — They are poorly off.

Schmecken. — Schmeckt Ihnen die Suppe nicht? — Do you not like that soup?

Er ist krank; ihm will nichts schmecken. — He is ill; he has no relish for anything.

Schon.—Bist du schon fertig? — Have you done already?

Das hätten Sie schon thun können. — You might certainly have done that.

Ich werde ihn schon überreden. — Never fear; I shall persuade him.

Schon gut! — Very well!

Das ist schon recht; aber ich habe das Geld nicht dazu. — That is all very well, but I have not got the money for it.

Schon sein Gang zeigt seinen Stolz. — His very gait shows his pride.

Schön. — Schönsten Dank! — Many thanks!

Die schöne Welt ist im Park zu sehen. — The fashionable world is to be seen in the park.

Der Pastor hat ein schönes Alter erreicht. — The Rector has attained to a good old age.

Er giebt gern schöne Worte. — He is fond of giving fair words.

Sie thut mit ihnen schön. — She is fondling them.

Schonen (sich). — Der Patient muß sich schonen. — The patient must take care of himself.

Schooß. — Er legt die Hände in den Schooß. — He is doing nothing.

Schreiben. — Wie schreiben Sie sich? — How do you spell your name?

Schreiben Sie sich das hinters Ohr! — Take notice of that!

Schrot. — Er ist ein Mann von gutem Schrot und Korn. — He is a man of sterling value.

Schuh. — Das wollte er mir in die Schuhe schieben. — He tried to lay the fault on me.

Schuld. — Die Schuld liegt an Ihnen. — It is your fault.

Er hat sich einen groben Fehler zu Schulden kommen lassen.	He has been guilty of gross misdemeanour.
Schule. — Der Knabe ging neben die Schule.	The boy played the truant.
Er hat schon öfters die Schule geschwänzt.	He has repeatedly shirked school.
Schuß. — Es kam mir heute nichts in den Schuß.	Nothing came within the range of my gun to-day.
Schütze. — Er ist ein niefehlender Schütze.	He is a dead shot.
Schwärmt. — Alles schwärmt für ihn.	Everybody is madly fond of him.
Er schwärmt für Musik und Malerei.	He is enthusiastically fond of music and painting.
Schwarz. — Das sollen Sie schwarz auf weiß haben.	You shall have it in writing.
Er hat das Schwarze getroffen.	He hit the bull's eye.
Schweißfuchs. — Mein Vater hat einen Schweißfuchs gekauft. (151)	My father has bought a light bay horse.
Schwer. — Diese Bücher haben mich schweres Geld gekostet.	These books cost me a lot of money.

Sie macht ihm das Leben schwer.	She is making life a burden to him.
Das ist schwerverdientes Geld.	That is hard-gotten money.
Es kömmt ihn schwer an.	He finds it hard.
Sechs. — Er fährt mit Sechsen.	He drives a coach and six.
Segel. — Das Schiff ging unter Segel.	The ship set sail.
Er ließ die Matrosen die Segel streichen.	He ordered the sailors to strike sail.
Segeln. — Vor dem Winde segelt sich's gut.	It is very nice running before the wind.
Sehen. — Sehen Sie gut?	Have you good sight?
Nein, ich sehe schlecht.	No, my sight is bad.
Er sieht darauf.	He sees to it.
Sieh mir ins Gesicht.	Look into my face.
Sie werden etwas zu sehen bekommen.	You will get sight of something.
Seite. — Die Preußen fielen den Östreichern in die Seite.	The Prussians took the Austrians in flank.
Ich lasse mich von der Seite photographieren.	I get photographed in profile.
Selbst. — Selbst unter gemeinen Leuten ist das anstößig.	Even amongst common people this is **offensive**.

Der Kaiser von Rußland ist ein Selbstherrscher. — The Emperor of Russia is an autocrat.

Selig. — Mein seliger Bruder liegt dort begraben. — My poor brother lies buried there.

Selten. — Das ist ein seltener Vogel. — That is a rare bird.

Er besucht uns sehr selten. — He comes to see us very rarely.

Setzen. — Was hat es gesetzt? — What has taken place?

Er ist ein gesetzter junger Mann. — He is a steady young man.

Sinken. — Er ließ den Mut sinken. — He lost courage.

Sinn. — Die arme Frau ist von Sinnen. — The poor woman is out of her mind.

Sinnig. — Das ist ein sehr sinniges Geschenk. — That is a very thoughtful present.

Sitzen. — Bleibt nur sitzen! — Stay where you are, I say!

Er ist sitzen geblieben. — He has not been promoted.

Sie ist sitzen geblieben. — She was a wallflower.

Da sitzt der Knoten. — There is the rub.

So. — Recht so! — That's the thing!

Nicht so! — That is not the way!

So? — Indeed!

So, das ist mir eine schöne Geschichte!	Why, that is a pretty piece of business!
So, das ist fertig.	Well, I am glad that is done.
Wie so?	How is that?
Soviel ich höre.	As far as I could learn.
Wenn du kannst, so komme.	If you are able *(then)* come.
Er ist nicht so dumm, wie sie glauben.	He is not so stupid as they think.
Wie gewonnen, so zerronnen.	Light come, light go.
Sollen.—Sie hätten es thun sollen.	You ought to have done so.
Wenn das Wetter sich ändern sollte.	If the weather were to change.
Ich sollte das thun?	I do that, never!
Sie sollen recht haben.	Well, I will allow you to be right.
Mein Bruder sollte Pastor werden.	My brother was to be a parson.
Was soll das Lachen?	What is the meaning of your laughter?
Wozu soll das?	What is the use of that?
Er soll in Paris sein.	They say he is in Paris.
Er soll sehr reich sein.	He is supposed to be very rich.

Soll und Haben.	Debtor and creditor.
Stehen.—Wie steht es mit Ihrer Gesundheit?	How is your health
Mit mir steht es schlecht.	I am in a bad way.
Wie steht es zu Hause?	How are they all at home?
Ich stehe zu Ihren Diensten.	I am at your service.
Stellen.—Es stellten sich siebzehn Kandidaten.	Seventeen candidates presented themselves.
Er stellt sich als ob er schliefe.	He is pretending to sleep.
Sie stellt sich taub.	She feigns to be deaf.
Der Junge stellt sich nur so.	The boy is humbugging.
Still. — Stille Wasser gründen tief. (152)	Still waters run deep.
Stimmen. — Das Lied stimmt mich immer fröhlich.	That song always puts me in good humour.
Das stimmt!	That is in keeping!
Das Instrument ist nicht gestimmt.	The instrument is out of tune.
Ich bin heute nicht gut gestimmt.	I am not up to the mark to-day.
Stroh.—Das heiße ich leeres Stroh dreschen.	I call these useless endeavours.
Ich bin gegenwärtig Strohwitwer.	My wife is away just now.

Suchen.—Das hätte ich nicht bei ihr gesucht. — I should not have thought she could do that.

Süß.—Die Forelle ist ein Süßwasserfisch. — The trout is a fresh-water fish.

T.

Tag.—Es ist noch sehr früh am Tage. — It is yet very early.

Der Arzt kam dreimal des Tages. — The doctor came three times a day.

Der Diebstahl wurde bei hellem Tage verübt. — The theft was committed in broad daylight.

Ich werde nächster Tage an ihn schreiben. — I shall write to him one of these days.

Heutzutage schreibt man nicht mehr so. — Nowadays you no longer spell so.

Tausend.—Das ist ein Märchen aus Tausend und Eine Nacht. (153) — That is a fairy tale from the Arabian nights.

Text.—Dem will ich den Text lesen. — I will give him a blow-up.

Thun.—Es ist mir um mein Kind zu thun. — I am anxious about my child.

Das thut nichts. — Never mind.

Der Name thut nichts zur Sache. — The name is nothing to the purpose.

Er that als ob er schliefe. — He pretended to sleep.

Tisch.—Bei Tische sprachen wir davon.	We spoke of it at dinner.
Vor Tische gehen wir in den Garten.	Before dinner we go into the garden.
Kommen Sie nach Tische.	Come after dinner.
Ich blieb bei dem Obersten zu Tische.	I stayed and dined with the colonel.
Tod.—Schweig oder du bist des Todes.	Be silent, or you are a dead man.
Der Pfarrer ist todkrank.	The rector is dangerously ill.
Ton.— Du hältst den Ton nicht.	You do not keep in tune.
Sie ist eine Dame von gutem Ton.	She is a gentlewoman.
Jene Familie giebt den Ton an.	That family are leading the fashion.
Tragen (sich). — Sie trägt sich mit eiteln Hoffnungen.	She is cherishing vain hopes.
Treffen.—Gut getroffen.	That was a good hit.
Sie sind gut getroffen.	That is a good likeness of yours.
Die Reihe trifft Sie.	It is your turn.
Du hast es bei ihr getroffen.	You did it to her mind.
Er schoß, aber er traf nichts.	He fired, but he missed.

Das trifft sich.	It happens to come at the right time.
Treffen.—Es kam zum Treffen.	There was an engagement.
Treiben.—Was treibst Du da. (154)	What are you doing there?
Es treibt mich nach Hause.	I long to go home.
Was trieb Sie so bald von dannen?	What made you leave there so soon?
Er treibt Botanik.	He is going in for botany.
Wie man's treibt, so geht's.	Do well, and have well.
Treten.—Treten Sie näher!	Come nearer!
Der Rhein trat über seine Ufer.	The Rhine overflowed its banks.
Treten Sie mir nie mehr unter die Augen.	Never appear before me any more.
Ich hatte mir einen Dorn in den Fuß getreten.	I had run a thorn into my foot.

U.

Übel.—Das wird ihr übel bekommen.	That will turn out badly for her.
Es wird mir übel.	I feel sick.
Das müssen Sie nicht übel nehmen.	You must not be offended at that.

über.—Ich reise über Köln nach Berlin. | I travel to Berlin by way of Cologne.

Übers Jahr ist er frei. | In a year he will be free.

Heute über acht Tage kommt mein Freund. | My friend will come this day week.

überein.—Darin komme ich mit Ihnen überein. | I agree with you in that.

Wir haben ein Übereinkommen getroffen. | We have entered into arrangements.

Überfluß.—Wir haben Überfluß an Büchern. | We have books in abundance.

überhaupt.—Wenn er überhaupt beistimmt. | If he consents after all.

übernehmen.—Er hat sich im Trunk übernommen. | He drank to excess.

Um.—(155) Er ist um drei Zoll größer als Sie. | He is taller than you by three inches.

Er kam um Weihnachten. | He came about Christmas.

Um so besser! | So much the better!

Umstand.—(156) Machen Sie keine Umstände. | Do not stand on ceremony.

Ohne viel Umstände. | Without much ado.

Umständlich.—Das ist mir viel zu umständlich. | That would give me too much trouble.

Unten.—Die Kinder sind unten.	The children are downstairs.
Du wirst es dort unten finden.	You will find it below there.
Unter. — Das geschah unter Karl dem Großen.	That happened in the reign of Charlemagne.
Das Feuer brach unter dem Gottesdienste aus.	The fire broke out during service.
Unter dem Donner der Kanonen zog der König in seiner Hauptstadt ein.	The king entered his capital amidst the roar of cannon.
Man fand den Schein unter seinen Papieren.	The certificate was found amongst his papers.

V.

Verdrießen.—Das verdroß mich.	That vexed me.
Wir ließen uns keine Mühe verdrießen.	We spared no pains.
Vergehen.—Es verging ihm Hören und Sehen.	He was quite stunned.
Vergreifen.—Das Werk ist vergriffen.	The work is out of print.
Verlegen.—Er war sehr verlegen.	He felt very small.
Voll.—Der Eimer war bis oben voll.	The bucket was brimful.

Die Halle war bis zum Erdrücken voll.	The hall was crowded to excess.
Er ist volle fünfzig Jahre alt.	He is full fifty.
Englisches Gold wird in Deutschland für voll angenommen.	English gold fetches full value in Germany.
Die Uhr hat voll geschlagen.	The clock struck the hour.
Er ist jetzt volljährig.	He is now of age.
Von.—Von da an wurde er immer schwächer. (157)	From that time he got weaker and weaker.
Von nun an speisen wir um sieben Uhr.	From henceforward we shall dine at seven.
Das lernt man von Kindesbeinen auf.	That you learn in your early childhood.
Vor.—Es geschah vor acht Tagen.	It happened a week ago.
Vor allem, seien Sie vorsichtig.	Above all, be cautious.
Er zitterte vor Furcht.	He trembled with fear.
Er hat einen Abscheu vor Trunkenbolden.	He has a horror of drunkards.
Vorkommen. — Die Pflanze kommt hier nicht vor.	That plant is not met with here.
Die Angelegenheit kam heute nicht vor.	The matter was not touched upon to-day.

Es kömmt mir vor, als wäre ich zehn Jahre jünger.	I feel ten years younger.
Ich weiß nicht, wie Sie mir heute vorkommen.	I do not know what to make of you to-day.
Vorläufig.—Sagen Sie vorläufig nichts.	Do not say anything for the present.

W.

Wahr.—Nicht wahr, Sie kommen?	You will come, will you not?
Wasser.—Sie siegten zu Wasser und zu Lande.	They were victorious by sea and by land.
Das heiße ich Wasser ins Meer tragen.	That is what I call carrying coals to Newcastle.
Das Wasser läuft mir im Munde zusammen.	My mouth waters.
Wechseln.—Können Sie mir diese Banknote wechseln?	Can you change this bank-note for me?
Wir wechseln Briefe mit einander.	We correspond.
Sie wechselten Worte mit einander.	They were quarrelling.
Weg.—Hier geht kein Weg durch.	There is no thoroughfare.
Das hat gute Wege.	There is no danger.
Machen Sie sich schnell auf den Weg.	Set off quickly.

Weh.—Ihm thut der Kopf weh. — His head aches.

Weibchen.—Da ist ein Kanarienvogel mit seinem Weibchen. — There is a canary with his mate.

Wein.—Wir saßen bei einem Glase Wein. — We sat over a glass of wine.

Es war gerade Weinlese, als ich den Rhein hinauffuhr. — There was just the vintage going on when I was travelling up the Rhine.

Weis.—Machen Sie mir das nicht weis. (158) — Do not try to make me swallow that.

Weiß.—Der Sonntag nach Ostern heißt in Deutschland Weißer Sonntag (159.) — The Sunday after Easter (Low Sunday) is in Germany called "White" Sunday.

Er zog weiße Wäsche an. — He changed his linen.

Weit.—Habe ich noch weit nach London? — Is it a long way yet to London?

Diese Matte ist bei weitem nicht so gut als jene. — This mat is not nearly so good as that.

Warum fährst du nicht weiter? — Why are you not going on?

Welchen, welche, welches (meaning *some*)—Haben Sie Postpapier? — Have you any note-paper?

Ja, ich habe welches.	Yes, I have some.
Welt. — Was in aller Welt soll das heißen?	What, I wonder, can be the meaning of that?
Die junge Welt will unterhalten sein.	Youth will be amused.
Ich war in beiden Welten.	I was in both hemispheres.
Er ist ehrlich, aber er hat keine Welt.	He is honest, but he has no manners.
Er ist ein Mann von Welt.	He is a man of the world.
Werden. — Das Werk ist im Werden.	The work is being done.
Dazu kann Rat werden.	That may be remedied.
Aus Kindern werden Leute.	Children become men and women.
Was wird aus dem Kinde werden?	What will become of the child?
Daraus kann nichts werden.	That is quite out of the question.
Wie ward es weiter?	What took place after?
Werfen. — Er warf mir ein Loch in den Kopf.	He cut my head by throwing a stone at me.
Man muß nicht mit Schimpfwörtern um sich werfen.	One must not call people bad names.
Er wirft sich auf Naturwissenschaften und Mathematik.	He is taking up science and mathematics.

Werk.—Es ist etwas im Werke.	There is something in the wind.
Wettrennen. (160.) — Es wurde ein Wettrennen gehalten.	A race was run.
Wie.—Wie so?	How is that?
Er wird schon kommen; wie anders?	He is sure to come; why should he not?
Wieviel Uhr ist es?	What is the time?
Um wieviel Uhr fährt der Zug ab?	At what time does the train start?
Den wievielten haben wir heute?	What is the day of the month?
Der wievielte war dieser Kandidat?	What was the place of this candidate?
Wo. (161.)— Jetzt, wo alle Stellen übersetzt sind.	Now when all places are overcrowded.
Wohl. — Mir ist nicht wohl zu Mute.	I do not feel comfortable.
Das that mir wohl.	That did me good.
Er blieb wohl eine Woche aus.	He was absent nearly a week.
Es mochten deren wohl hundert gewesen sein.	There might have been about a hundred.
Wollen. — Davon will ich nichts wissen.	I will have nothing to do with the matter.
Sei es, was es wolle.	Whatever it may be.

Z.

Zeug. (162.)—Dazu hat er nicht das Zeug. — He is not fit for it.

Das ist lauter dummes Zeug. — That is all stuff and nonsense.

Sind Sie schon im Zeughause (163) gewesen? — Have you been at the arsenal?

Ziehen.—Er zieht den Kopf aus der Schlinge. — He is backing out of that affair.

Er zog den Kürzern. — He was the loser.

Wir zogen sie ins Geheimnis. — We let her into the secret.

Der Krieg zog sich in die Länge. — The war was protracted.

Napoleon zog nach Rußland. — Napoleon marched into Russia.

Es zieht in diesem Zimmer. — There is a draught in this room.

Es zieht nicht. — It is no go.

Das zieht bei mir nicht. — That will not take with me.

Zug. (164.)—Der Knabe lag in den letzten Zügen. — The boy was dying.

Nimm kleine Züge, mein Kind. — Take small draughts, my child.

Das Kamin hat keinen Zug. — The chimney does not draw.

Wir lesen Alexanders Zug nach Indien.	We read Alexander's march to India.
Er fährt mit dem letzten Zuge.	He starts by the last train.
Wir fuhren mit dem Schnellzuge.	We travelled by the fast train.
Das ist ein guter Zug an ihr.	That is a good point in her character.

NOTES.

Page
1 (1) **Ab.** Lat. *ab.* Gk. *ἀπό*, Sanscrit *apa*. An old root with the meaning of from, or out from, proceeding from. The Scandinavian *af* and the English *of* are kindred words according to Grimm's Law.

(2) Compare the English *off and on*, which, although meaning a different thing from the idiom quoted, still helps to remember it, owing to its similar construction.

(3) Word formed from ab = off, and fertig = ready.

2 (4) The German also is like the English *also*, simply the word so intensified by all (al). But in derivations a beginner cannot be sufficiently cautioned against the wrong impression that a word must mean the same thing with another, because it is derived from the same root. Appearances are deceptive, and in the case in hand the English student must never confound the German also with English *also*. The German also means *thus, so, in this manner, so far, consequently, therefore*, whilst the English *also* is the German auch, gleichfalls, ebenfalls, dazu.

(5) Never say, London liegt auf der Themse, Brighton auf dem Meere (a very common mistake made by English learners of German, originating in the fact that *on* in English means both *close to* and *on top of*). Auf, with the dative case, means simply *on the top or surface of*. Thus we say: Sie lag auf dem Sofa. She was lying on the sofa. Er stand auf dem Berge. He stood on the top of the mountain. Wir waren auf dem Meere. We were out at sea.

Page
4 (6) **Auch.** Old High German *ouh, auh* and *ouch* Gothic *auk*, Anglo-Saxon *eac*, English *eke*:
('Twill be prodigious hard to prove,
That this is *eke* the throne of love),
Prior.
in addition, also, likewise — are connected with the roots of the words augēre (Latin), and αὔξειν and αὐξάνειν (Greek), which both mean to make to grow, to increase, and consequently to *add*. Grimm's Law again bears out the fact.

7 (7) **Bar** (old spelling baar). Old High Germ. *par*, Middle High Germ. *bar*, belongs to the same root with our English *bear* = to bring forth. Our *bare*, uncovered, naked, is the same word. The German barfuß, barhaupt, barefoot, bareheaded, show that. From thence the sense of *distinctly seen* (as cash paid down is) is clearly derivable. *Rückert* has the pun, Ihr geleitet die Bahre und denkt dabei an das Bare. You accompany the coffin, and at the same time think of the cash. Diese zweitausend Thaler hier blank und bar auf meinem Tisch. These 2000 Thalers down in cash on my table. *Tieck.*

(8) **Einen Bären aufbinden.** The word aufbinden in the phrase einem etwas aufbinden, *to make one believe what is not true*, is quite sufficient. Compare Latin *imponere alicui aliquid*. *Weigand* says aufbinden, in our meaning, comes from the custom of tying presents to one's arm or sleeve, formerly much in vogue.

When used figuratively it would mean to hoax one by tying there something mean or worthless. Why the *bear* should have been chosen as that worthless thing is not quite clear.

Werdet ihr meinen, ich sei ganz dumm und man könne mir Bären aufbinden, einen ganzen Bärengraben voll. *Gotthelf.*

(9) **Um des Kaisers Bart streiten** or **zanken**, that is disputing about a thing utterly unattainable. (*Weigand*).
Um des Kaisers Bart zanken, sagt man von unnötigem, kleinlichem, vergeblichem Streit. (*Sanders.*)
French: *Se disputer de la chape à l'évêque.* Se

Page		
7	(10)	**Bedienen Sie sich.** Compare the French *Servez-vous.*
	(11)	**Was befehlen Sie?** French *Que commandez-vous?*
8	(12)	**Sich befinden** = French *Se trouver.*
	(13)	**Begreifen** = to get the grip of something. Exactly the meaning of Latin *comprehendere.*
	(14)	**Begriffen sein** = to be at or about a thing, to have it just in hand. French, *être en train de.*
	(15)	**Bei.** Be careful not to translate the English *by* by the German word *bei* when it means through, as author, maker, or cause, or whenever in Latin it would be rendered by *a*, *ab*, *per*, or the French *par*. In that case *by* means **von** or **durch**. When *by* means *close by*, *near* or *during*, it is often given by **bei**. Thus **beim Graben**, by the ditch; **beim Bahnhof**, near the railway station; **bei Tage, bei Nacht**, by day, by night.
9	(16)	**Betrieb** from the verb **betreiben**, originally *to be driving something, making it go*, hence the sense *of carrying it on, working it.* Compare **Betriebs-material**, rolling stock, **Betriebskapital**, working capital, **Betriebskosten,** working expenses.
	(17)	**Blank.** This word is not taken from French or any other Romance language. It is just the reverse. It is in Old High Germ. *blanch*, Anglo-Saxon *blonc*, Dutch, Danish, Swedish and English *blank*. The original meaning is a *brilliant white or pale colour.* **Blinken**, the verb, meaning to *sparkle, gleam, shimmer, glitter*, explains the meaning of our idiom. French *blanc*, Span. *blanco*, Port. *branco*, It. *bianco.*
	(18)	**Blauen Montag machen.** According to Weigand, from the custom of hanging the Churches in blue on the Monday before Ash Wednesday, when there being Carnival time in Roman Catholic countries,

(continued from previous) dit de gens se disputant d'une chose qui ne leur appartient pas et qu'ils ne doivent point obtenir. *Littré.* Italian: *Disputare dell' ombra dell' asino.*

holiday making and frolicking were the order of the day.

9 (19) **Ins Blaue schwatzen.** To speak into empty (blue) air, without any definite purpose, or without knowing what, just as one who beats the air without hitting anything.

10 (20) This is a queer idiom. *Weigand* says it means so to be driven to bay that the victim should like to squeeze himself into a goat's horn. "Der hat ihn ins Bocksdorn gejagt". *(Gœthe.)*

(21) **Bodensee.** It was formerly called der Bobmersee, from a castle and village of Bobman lying on its northwestern arm. It is sometimes called das Schwäbische Meer. Konstanz belongs to the Grand Duchy of Baden, consequently to Germany, although lying on the Swiss side of this magnificent sheet of water.

(22) **Bringen** means not only *to bring*, but also *to get, to take, to carry*.

11 (23) **Busen,** Latin *sinus*, which also has both meanings, and so has the Greek word κόλπος, Old High German *puosum* and *puosam*, Middle High Germ. *buosem*. Engl. *bosom*. The word is thought to be connected with bauschen, to swell like a full bag, to protrude.

(24) **Wer da?** Stands for Wer ist da? or Wer geht da? Note the word Schildwache, *sentry*, which is feminine in German as in French. Wache, *watch*, is feminine, and the word, following the rule of all compounds, takes its gender from the last component. It means a warrior in complete armour, shield in hand. The word is met with in that sense in the great German Epic of the Nibelungen. It is there called "Schiltwahte".

(25) **Dafür.** Notice that, owing to the grammatical impossibility in German, of joining the neuter pronoun of the third person to a preposition, a substitute is called for, and this substitute is the Adverb da (before a vowel it reassumes the older form dar), which is placed immediately before the preposition.

Page		
11		**John Earle**, in his *Philology of the English Tongue*, calls words so formed *Flexional Pronoun Adverbs*. (Thus we have *thereat, thereby, therefor, therefore, therefrom, therein,* and many others.) In I. Kings VII. 27, *whereof* is used interchangeably with *of it*. "And he made ten bases of brass; four cubits was the length, of one base and four cubits the breadth *thereof*, and three cubits the height *of it*." The same author presents these Composites in the form of a declension:

        Nom. that *or* it.
        Gen. thereof.
        Dat. thereto *or* therefor (e).
        Acc. that *or* it.
        Abl. therefrom.
        Instr. thereby.

Da is in Old High German *dar, thar* and *dara*, in Anglo-Saxon *thær*, in Dutch *daar*.

13 (26) **Dasig** stands for baig or barig. S was the proper consonant, as it often stands for *r*. Compare *hare* and Hase. Thus we have hiesig for hierig.

14 (27) **Desto besser.** The Latin *tanto melius*, and the French *tant mieux*. Desto is in Old High German *dêsdiû*, Middle High German *deste* — In Luther's writings we find beste.

(28) **Deutsch reden.** *Cicero* in *Verrem, de Signis*, has: "*Latine* me scitote, non accusatorie loqui" — where *latine* is the equivalent of our "*in plain English*."

15 (29) **Drittehalb** and **dritthalb**. We have vierthalb, fünfthalb. The explanation is, first come two, three or four wholes, then the fraction as the third, fourth or fifth in order. Never say zweithalb or zweitehalb, but anderthalb for one and a half.

(30) **Der, die, das drittletzte** = The third when counting from the end.

(31) **Dürfen.** Remember also that the *Past Participles* gekonnt, gewollt, gemocht, gemüßt, gesollt and gedurft become **können, wollen, mögen, müssen, sollen, dürfen,** whenever they are preceded by the infinitive of another verb; as **ich habe gehen dürfen.** I

was allowed to go; whilst *I was allowed* would be ich habe gedurft. (Becker's First German Book, p. 88) Compare the following sentences given by *Daniel Sanders* in his "*Deutsches Wörterbuch*" — where he quotes also other similar verbs taking no zu before the Infinitive: Er hat mich gehen heißen; mir tragen helfen; mich kommen hören; ausgehen können; ihn schreiben lassen; lesen lernen; nicht essen mögen; uns gehen sehen; gestern kommen sollen; nicht kommen wollen.

16 (32) **Eben.** Gothic *ibns*, Old High German *ëpan*, Middle High German *ëben*, Engl. *even*. When it means *level, smooth*; *exactly, actually, so much*, it agrees in meaning with the English word.

"Den eben suche ich" — is by *Gœthe*.

"Wie ging's? . . ." Nicht eben allzugut. *Wieland*.

Ich war eben darauf bedacht . . . . , als ich Ihren Brief erhielt. *Lessing*.

(33) **Ei** has like **so** and **ja** many shades of meaning. It expresses surprise, admiration, applause, vexation, impatience, entreaty, encouragement, reproach, doubt, hesitation. *Sanders* says it is "Ein Naturlaut," and compares it with ah, ai, eh, ie. English equivalents: *why*! (interjection), *I never*! (detto), *well*, well done, *pshaw*. The tone in which ei is pronounced must determine the meaning.

„Ei, du frommer und getreuer Knecht!" Matth. 25. 21. „Ei, das ist ja ein Wallensteiner." Ei, wie geputzt! *Goethe, Schiller*.

(34) **Eigen.** This word has all the meanings of the Greek word ἴδιος. namely, 1. *one's own, personal, private*. 2. *peculiar, separate, distinct, strange*. Es ist um einen großen Mann eine eigne Sache. *Immermann*. Das eigne Wesen des Jünglings fiel dem Grafen bald auf. *Kerner*.

(35) **Eigentlich** — originally = *particularly, distinctly*. Anglo-Saxon *âgendlice*, Middle High Germ. eigenliche. So ist es mir eigentlich nur um den Wortverstand zu thun. *Goethe*.

(36) **Eile haben.** French *avoir hâte*. Compare *avoir*

Page		
		soif, avoir faim, avoir honte, avoir envie, avoir peur, avoir froid, avoir chaud.
16	(37)	**Ein** is here an adverb.
17	(38)	**Einrücken** = *to shove or move into*, which will bear out the present meaning in the idiom.
	(39)	Compare in Meissner's Public School Grammar (Hachette & Co.) the chapters on the derivation of German Verbs, pp. 178 & ff.
18	(40)	**Weil.** Notice the meaning in the idiom. It ought now to be used in the sense of "*because*", but was formerly, and *is* still occasionally, used as an adverb of time.

„Weil ich fern bin, führe du
 Mit klugem Sinn das Regiment des Hauses".
      Schiller, Wilhelm Tell.
„Nie ging ihm, weil er lebt geschwinder
 Die Arbeit von der Faust". *Wieland.*

19	(41)	**Entgegengehen** is exactly the French *aller au devant.*
	(42)	**Erbitten.** The prefix **er** gives the verb the meaning of *growing or obtaining* what the verb expresses, as: erröten, to blush, erhalten, to obtain, erbitten, to obtain by prayers.
	(43)	**Ergreifend** = Fch. *saisissant* in exactly the same sense.
20	(44)	**Eule** is connected with the Latin *úlula* = *barn owl*; Anglo-Saxon *eovle*, later *ûle*, Engl. *owl*, Old Norse & Swedish *ugla*, Danish *ugle*. The German idiom is the Greek saying γλαῦκ' 'Ἀθήναζε, γλαῦκ εἰς 'Ἀθήνας. The owl, as is well known, was the favourite bird of Minerva, *Gk.* Athene. — The Athenian coins bore the stamp of the owl on them.
	(45)	The Latin *extrema se tangunt* — French *les extrêmes se touchent.*
21	(46)	**Fabrik*** Never take this word to mean the English *fabric*. This would be Fabrikat, Gewebe, Zeug in German. The word Fabrik is directly derived from the Latin *fábrica* = *workshop*. The French *la fabrique* has, of course, the same origin, and corresponds exactly with the German meaning of the word.

  *** Put the stress on the last syllable.*

Page
21 (47) **Fach** = *division of some space* — hence "ein Mann von Fach", a man versed in some special department. The root is connected with *Gk*. πήγνυναι, and *Lat*. pangere, to fix or arrange. „Er fragte jeden nach seinem Fache und äußerte, daß man streng auf Fächer halten müßte." *Goethe.*

(48) **Fahren** = *to drive or be driven.* In English sometimes *to ride* is used in this sense. The kindred German word reiten must only be used of riding on the back of an animal.

22 (49) **Nötigenfalles** may be styled a Genitive absolute.

23 (50) **Fällen** means literally to fell, *to cause to fall to the ground*; then also *to cast, to let go, to let fall.* The latter meanings will help to explain the idiom. As to the formation of the word from fallen, see *Meissner's Public School Grammar*, 45th Lesson.

(51) **Sie singt falsch** = French *elle chante faux.*

24 (52) **Das reimt sich**, etc. About the English word "rhyme," as usually spelt in this saying, Earle says in his *Philology of the English Tongue* already quoted: "Too many cases remained in which the *y* had become fixed in places where an *i* should have been. A *conspicuous example* is the word *rhyme*, which is from the Saxon word *rîm*, number. Possibly the *y* was put for *i* from confusion with the Greek ρυθμός, rhythmos. From the above will be seen that our words Reim and reimen are the cousins of *rim* and *riman* in Anglo-Saxon. As for the idiom itself, it may be compared with French "*Cela rime comme hallebarde et miséricorde.*"— It is only a pity we have not to offer such a good story for our German idiom. See *Henri Bué, First Steps in French Idioms* p. 105. Faust is in Old High German *fûst*, and an old relative of Lat. *pugnus* and Gk. πύξ, and Slav *pjastj.* (*Webster*). Instead of das reimt sich, we can also say, das paßt wie die Faust aufs Auge.

(53) **Feiern.** Latin *feriari* — Thus *Horace*: male *feriatos* Troas, keeping *holiday* at an unseasonable time.

„Nicht lang gefeiert! frisch! die Mauersteine herbei!" *Schiller*, W. T.

Page		
24	(54)	**Fein** — (not *coarse, delicate, tender, thin*). According to *Diez, Wbch.* our word is borrowed from *Fch. fin*, which in *Ital.* and *Span.* is *fino*, and is derived from *finitus*. We might call a delicate texture *well finished*. Even in Classical Latin finītus has that meaning. So *Cicero* uses the word of *well rounded phrases*.
25	(55)	**Feind.** Er ist ihm feind = *Lat. inimicus est illi.* Seine Brüder waren ihm feind. Gen. 37. 4. (*Luther's* Transl.)
	(56)	**Fell** is ordinarily only used of the skin of animals; the human skin is Haut.
	(57)	**Ferien** — Latin Cic. *feriæ* — Zeit des Feierns in Schulen und Gerichten. (*Sanders.*)
	(58)	**Fiaker** — from the French *fiacre*. *Brachet* in his Et. D. of the Fch. L. has the following explanation of this word. *Fiacre, sm.*, a hackney coach, cab; a word of historic origin: it dates from A. D. 1640, when the first carriages for hire were stationed in Paris at the Hotel St. Fiacre. Ménage wrote in 1650: Fiacre —"On appelle ainsi à Paris depuis quelques années un carosse de louage, à cause de l'image de Saint Fiacre qui pendait pour enseigne à un logis de la rue Saint Antoine, où on louait ces sortes de carosses. C'est dont je suis témoin oculaire".

„Die Fiaker, die sie hier (in Berlin) Droschken heißen". *Auerbach.*

| | (59) | **Fideles Haus,** for jolly good fellow. University slang. We call the partners of a firm, or the Parliament assembled *a house*. |

„Ein sogenanntes fideles Haus". *Klencke.*
„Herr Bruder sei heut kreuzfidel". *Liederbuch.*

| 26 | (60) | **Fidibus.** Gen. Fidibusses, Pl. Fidibusse — A strip of paper for lighting pipes or cigars, occurs first about the middle of the 17th century. It appears to have had its origin (like the word above) at the Universities; but why it came to be called so, has not yet been satisfactorily settled. The conjectures which have been made are too fanciful for repetition. |

„Zur Not könnten die lieben Herren Fidibusse daraus machen". *Chr. Weise.*

Page
26 (61) **Fischbein,** in full „Walfischbein", from the mistaken notion that the whale was a fish. „Die Unkunde... scheidet den Wal den Fischen zu". *Linck.* Fischbein now *never* means fish bone — *That* is Gräte (*f.*) in German.

(62) **Flächeninhalt** — Composed of Fläche, *surface,* and Inhalt, *extent.*

(63) **Flau** = *weak, feeble, soft, dull, dead,* from the *Dutch flaauw,* which has the same signification, and is ultimately connected with *flaccus* and flaccidus, from which we have the English word *flaccid* = flabby, soft, yielding.

(64) **Fleck** = spot.
„Es ist nur e i n Ort in der Welt! Wo er bestattet liegt . . .
Der einz'ge Fleck ist mir die ganze Erde". *Schiller.*

27 (65) **Flott** is both *adj.* and *adv.* and might here be explained by our English *swimmingly.*
„Ein flottes Fest ist unser Recht". *Goethe.*
„Daß wir flott und lustig leben". *Schiller.*

(66) **Flurschütz** = *Fch.* garde champêtre.

28 (67) **Davon ist jetzt nicht die Frage.** *Fch.* Il ne s'agit pas de cela.

(68) **Fragselig.** The word „selig," happy, is thus used with Leute, and forms leutselig, sociable, with reden it makes redselig, talkative, affable.

(68a) **Freitag** — **Karfreitag** — from O.H.G. *chara* = lamentation, wail, and *Friatac;* M.H.G. *Karfritac.* *Chara* is in Gothic *Kara,* and in Anglo-Saxon *cearu, caru* = care, grief, sorrow, lamentation; our English *care.* The name is evidently derived from the lamentations sung by the Church on that day in commemoration of the sufferings and death of Christ. In some Passion Plays, Mary was made to sing a dirge at the foot of the cross.

(69) **In der Fremde** = *Fch.* à l'étranger.

(70) **Fressen.** Do not use this word of mankind. The idiom, literally, *"Bird eat or die"* explains itself.
„Vogel friß oder stirb! Wer nicht mitmachen wollte, war des Lebens nicht sicher". *Hebel.*

Page
29 (71) **Frohn** = The word is very old. In Old High German *frono* meant "*belonging to the Lord*" or *Master*. It corresponds in meaning to the *Gk.* κυριακός, and the *Latin* dominicus. The R. Catholics call Corpus Christi Day das **Frohnleich**=**namsfest** = *Body of the Lord's Day* — **Leichnam** meaning *body*.

(72) **Funkelnagelneu, Funken,** *spark,* was in M.H.G. Funkels. The word literally means *glittering like a new nail.* — Compare spick (nail) — and span (chip).

30 (73) **Furore machen** — *Italian,* far furore. Ha fatto furore, he created a sensation. „Die große Furore, bie er hier erregt." *Heine.*

(74) **Vier Fuß lang** — Masculine or neuter nouns indicating weight or measure remain unchanged when preceded by numerals. Thus we have: Sechs Zoll, six inches; drei Pfund, three pounds — but fünf Ellen, five yards, because Elle is feminine.

(75) **Lebt** — „leben" would be wrong, Familie being in the Singular Number. We are not allowed to construe according to the sense in such cases. Thus in *French*: la famille *a* un grand train de maison.

(76) **Hat,** see 75. *Fch.* La cavalerie *vient* de fourrager.

31 (77) **Gabelfrühstück,** literally translated from the French *déjeuner à la fourchette.* It is not a German institution.

(78) **Lief ihm** über — Ethic Dative — Like Latin, "*Quid mihi Celsus agit?*" *Fch.* On lui a échauffé la bile, for sa bile, which an Englishman would expect.

32 (79) The suffix **bar** besides the meaning of *bearing* (frucht**bar**), expresses either what *will bear* doing, or what *can* or *may* be done. Thus it means here what will bear circulation or can or may be circulated or "uttered," according to the Law Term.

(80) In „iß, was **gar** ist," we have the original meaning of gar, which is *ready.* From *ready* the other meanings, *altogether, completely, quite,* can easily

be derived. O. H. G. *Karawo, garawo, karo* and *garo* — Old Norse *gerr, giörr* (gjörr), *geyrr* = ready, ready made. Hence the meaning of *cooked ready for eating*. So we have: Der Gänſebraten und die Kartoffeln — ſind jetzt gar. The roast goose and the potatoes are ready now.

32 (81) **Gaſſenhauer** = gemeines Gaſſenlied (*Weigand*).

33 (82) **Gebildete** = literally *formed* — Those whose mind has been formed.

34 (83) **Gediegen** = literally *native, virgin, without admixture, pure*. O.H.G. *Kidikan* and *gidikan*.

(84) **Gefallen,** as a noun means originally the same with „Fall," the *Lat.* casus. As a verb it means *to fall in with one's wishes*, hence to please. The noun is evidently formed from the Infinitive „gefallen," which is demonstrable from the form „das Gefallen," which form is of comparatively recent occurrence.

(85) **Gefälligſt** is an adverb, but we have no exact equivalent in one word for it.

35 (86) **Gegend** is derived from gegen in the same manner as *Ital.* la contrada and *Fch.* la contrée = country, neighbourhood, are derived from *Lat.* contra = over against, on the opposite side, facing one.

(87) **Es geht auf Leben und Tod** — Compare the French — Il y va de la vie, life is at stake.

(88) **Gehört** = *Lat.* pertinet belongs to. Illa res ad meum officium pertinet. *Cic.*

(89) **Geige** = violin. The saying literally means: "For him the sky is studded with violins". The word Geige occurs in German as early as the 12th century. It is of French origin. We find it in Old and Modern Fch. *la gigue*, Provençal *gigua*, Ital. *giga*.

36 (90) **Geiſtlich** = ghostly, *in our ghostly counsel, ghostly Father* etc. *Lat.* spiritualis. Der Geiſtliche, ein Geiſtlicher, are like der Reiſende, der Geſandte, der Gelehrte, nouns made of adjectives, and therefore

Page		
		variable according to the article, pronoun or numeral preceding them.
		„Die Mönche gehören zu den Geistlichen, obwohl sie keine Priester sind". (*Sanders.*)
36	(91)	**Heu,** wie Heu = as plentiful as hay. „Geld wie Heu (d. h. in Fülle) haben". *Sanders.*
	(92)	**Gelegen** = convenient, fit, proper, seasonable, *Fch. à propos.* The idiom implies that, whether the matter be seasonable or not, it is of so little importance, that it will not make any difference.
37	(93)	**Gelten** = to be of value — O. H. G. këltan, A. S. gëldan, gieldan, gyldan. Latin *valēre.* Gelten machen is exactly the French *faire valoir.*
	(94)	**Gemäß** from messen, to measure, means *commensurate* — A. S. gemét. What meets the case.
38	(95)	"*The straight way is the best*". Read the amusing comedy by *Kotzebue* „Der gerade Weg, der beste".
	(96)	The Verb geraten (formerly spelt gerathen), Past. geriet, P. Part. geraten = glücken, to succeed, hence we say of *things* either es ist mir geraten, or geglückt.
	(97)	Compare Meissner, p. 206.
39	(98)	**Gern** = Goth. gairns; O. H. G. gërno; M.H.G. gërne. The Comparative is lieber; the Sup. am liebsten. Yet also gerner and am gernsten are met with. Thus Chamisso has „und gerner sich sonnen am Klarblick deiner Augen"; and Schiller, „Ich hab euch immer am gernsten gehabt". The Verb gehren, and the English *yearn* are of the same origin.
42	(99)	**Gnade** — O. H. G. ginâde. — The word means originally *stooping, condescension,* and is connected with nahen.
		„Ich wollte mich auf Ihre Gnade und Ungnade zu Ihren Füßen werfen". *Tieck.*
43	(100)	**Gönnen** — O. H. G. gunnan — M. H. G. gunnen — composed of the prefix *ge* and *unnan,* to wish well to some one.
	(101)	**Grauen.** — Compare *Goethe,* „Heinrich, mir graut's vor dir!"
44	(102)	Exactly the *French:* tu as beau dire. — Compare *Goethe,* "Aber man hat gut reden, gut sich und andern raten".

K

NOTES.

46 (103) **Hagestolz.** O. H. G. *hagastalt* and *hagustalt* = unmarried. It originally meant an unmarried servant (*m.*) living on a fenced round small estate. Components: *hag*, hedge, fence, and (*Goth.*) *stald* (*ans*), possessing (*Weigand*).

48 (104) The Fch. *penchant* means exactly the German **Hang.**

(105) **Purzelbaum** is also spelt **Burzelbaum**, derived from burzeln or purzeln, to stretch upward what has naturally a downward bent, and bäumen, to rear.

For **Hanswurst** we have an English word, *Jack Pudding* and the French *Jean Potage*. The German word first appeared in a Low German form early in the 16th century. As representing the clown in a theatre the name of **Hanswurst** is to be seen in a play acted in 1573. (*Weigand.*)

(106) **Hapern** = to stop, to be at a standstill.
„Mit bem Französischen haperte es etwas." (*Heine.*)
„Bei ben Ausgängen, hapert's" (*Heinse.*)
„Daran fürcht ich, möcht'es hapern" (*Goethe.*)

(107) Luther is very partial to this idiom throughout his writings. The word **Harnisch**, *armour*, was M.H.G. both *das* and *der harnasch* and *harnasch, harnisch, hernisch*, and *härnesch*, and was borrowed from O. F. *harnas, harnais*, and *harnois*, which again is derived from the Celtic *haiarnaez*, iron implements, a derivative of the Cymric haiarn (Old Breton) hoiarn, = iron. (*Weigand & Sanders.*)

„David wird sich nicht gerne haben wider ben Sohn aufbringen lassen, aber seine Hauptleute haben ihn bazu berebet und ihn in Harnisch gebracht". (*Luther*).

(108) *Nicolai & Schiller* have also ba liegt, ba stect der Hase im Pfeffer in the same sense.

49 (109) Literally to "seize the hares' banner". The fact that the hare is a very timid animal explains the idiom. French *prendre de la poudre d'escampette*.

51 (110) **Heißen,** intrans. with the name uninflected in the Nominative Case; to be called. Compare Chaucer's *highte* or *hyghte*, was called. A. S. hatan, to be named (*Skeat*).

NOTES.

Page

51 (111) **Heller,** the smallest copper coin of Germany, quite out of use, may be translated by our English "doit". It was originally *Haller*, then *Häller*, and lastly became *Heller*. The full word was first *"haler phenning,"* which they in Mediæval Latin translated by *"denarius Hallensis,"* because it was coined at the free imperial town of *Hall* in *Swabia*. Even a "drey haller" (1618) was a very small coin. (*Weigand*). The word **Thaler** has a similar origin. The first thalers were coined at *Joachimsthal*, a mining town in northwestern Bohemia. Hans Sachs (1494—1576) speaks of a "Joachimsthaler" as given to some one in payment, and the full name was still in use long after him. (*Sanders.*) „Keinen roten Heller haben or wert sein." (*Sanders*). „Alle gaben ihr drei Heller zum besten = ließen Ihre Weisheit hören". *Willkomm.*

(112) **Her.** O. H. G. hëra, means *hither*. Die Hand her = (Reach) hither thine hand! herauf and heraus were O. H. G. hëra ûf and hëra ûz.

53 (113) **Heute,** O. H. G. hiutû, is a contraction analogous to the Latin *hodie* of hoc die, of hiûtagû (on this day). Thus heuer, from O. H. G. hiurû, contracted from hiûjârû (in this year).

(113a) **Hexe,** literally *hag, witch*, then roguish woman or girl. „Die Hexen zu dem Brocken ziehen." *Goethe.* Solch ein Hexchen ist geschwind. (*Uhland.*)

(114) **Hin** means always *away* from the speaker, *thither*. Hinfahrt, O. H. G. hinafart; M. H. G. hinevart and hinvart.

54 (115) **Hof** means *yard*, and as such in many cases *surrounds* a detached house; hence the idea of using it for what surrounds the moon. Our English halo, Gk. ἄλως, a threshing floor, gave from its round shape its name to the disk of the sun or moon, and later to the luminous circle surrounding them. (*Webster.*)

(116) **Holen** — to fetch — has its representatives in all Teutonic dialects. Thus: Dutch *halen*, Dan. *hale*, Sw. and Icel. *hala*, English *haul*, and it has even been adopted by most of the Romance lan-

132 NOTES.

Page

    guages: French *haler*, Span. *hallar*, Port. *alar*. O. H. G. h lôn and halón. M. H. G. *holn* and *holen* — according to Grimm's Law a kindred word to Lat. calare, to convoke (calare comitia, *Gell.*), and to Gk. καλεῖν, to call together. (*Webster* and *Weigand*).

55 (117) **Hüttenwerk** = works consisting of many huts or sheds (O. H. G. *hutta*; M. H. G. *hütte*, Comp. Gk. κεύθω, to cover, to hide. (*Sanders*.)

56 (118) From the French *Chevalier d'industrie*, a swindler. **Glücksritter** means very much the same.

57 (119) **Ja** — M. H. G. and O. H. G. jâ., Goth. ja, A. S. (by extension) gese, gise and gyse, hence *yes*. Most of our idioms will better stand the comparison of ja with *yea*; A. S. ge.

59 (120) **Jüngst** = Lat. novissimus; novissimo die, on the last day. Adverb = Lat. *nuper*. For first meaning— „Von Gemälden ist nur ein jüngstes Gericht bemerkenswert." *W. Humboldt*.

(121) **Kaiser** — Goth. *Kaisar*, O. H. G. *cheisar*, M. H. G. *Keiser* — derived from Lat. Cæsar, Gk. Καῖσαρ.

(122) **Kanzlei** and *chancery* are the same words, and come from the L. Lat. *cancellaria*, from *cancellus*, a grating or bar which divided the judgment-seat from the people. French *chancellerie*, chancellor's house or office. In German the word means any government office.

60 (123) The word is composed of **kaubern**, to gabble, and **welsch**, foreign. **Kaubern** alone is also sufficient. „Was der durcheinander welscht und kaubert." (*Tieck*.)

(124) **Kauen**, lit. chew. Die Nägel, Finger, Lippen kauen or b a r a n kauen. (*Sanders*.)

(125) **Kennen** is the French *connaître* in all its meanings; **wissen** is the French *savoir*.

65 (126) This idiom is probably derived from the mediæval custom of having a lover drawn up to one's room in a basket. An unwelcome suitor would be accommodated with a basket whose bottom would give way, and land the poor fellow below in the mud or ditch (*Weigand*). Afterwards simply a

NOTES.

basket without a bottom was sent in token of refusal.

66 (127) **Kuckuck** is euphemistically used for „Teufel." *Tieck* has this passage: „Pot3 Kuckuck! ist so ein hergebrachter Aufruf, wenn wir nicht gerade fluchen wollen."

68 (128) **Lassen** = let, leave, allow. With an infinitive of a verb preceding, it has the force of causing a thing to be done, having it done. In this sense it exactly agrees with the French idiom *faire faire*. Our present idiom would be, *Il vous faudrait faire relier ces livres*.

69 (129) The word **Leichdorn** means simply *flesh-thorn*. In Latin we have *clavus*, a nail, meaning also a *corn*. In Old Norse it is *likthorn*, Low Germ. *likdorn*. Compare 70. Hühnerauge is always heard in the South.

70 (130) **Lernen** = gelernt, so lassen for gelassen. etc. and other verbs to be found in Meissner's Publ. Sch. Gr. p. 123.

(131) **Gelernt** may be called a participial adjective, and compared with such English words as *gifted*, *ill-conditioned*, *landed*, *learned*, *monied*.

71 (132) **Lieb** — O. H. G. *liup*, Goth. *liubs*, A. S *leof*, Engl. *lief*, with a comparative *liefer*, still heard in West of England country districts.

72 (133) **Lösen.** O. H. G. *losan*, Goth. *láusjan* = to let loose, to set free; then also *to pay*, like Latin *solvere*.

78 (134) **Mut** in its original meaning agrees with our English *mood* or *disposition* of the mind or heart or soul. That will explain the idioms.

79 (135) **Der Nächste**, neighbour = *prochain*, Lat. *proximus*. Nachbar = local neighbour. Compare *prochain* and *voisin* in French.

83 (136) **Ohnmacht** from Ohne and Macht, without power or strength.

(137) **Ostern** — O. H. G. Ostrâ (Plur.) Luther also uses it in the plural number: „Die Ostern hat man vor bem Koncilio zu Nicäa auf eine andre Zeit gehalten." Thus we also have plural forms for Weihnachten, Christmas, and Pfingsten, Pentecost, Whitsuntide.

The word, which in Anglo-Saxon is *Eastre*, has the same derivation with the latter, *i. e.* from the name of a goddess of light or spring, in honour of whom a Festival was celebrated in April (*Webster*.)

84 (138) *Luther* refers to this idiom when he says,

„Er follt . . . Herr im Haufe fein, wenn die Frau nicht daheim ift und zum Zeichen zog er ihm einen Schuh aus und, legte ihn aufs Himmelbette, daß er die Herrschaft und das Regiment behielte."

Thus we also say, die Frau **hat, schwingt, führt** den Pantoffel.

87 (139) **Quer** — O. H. G. *twer*, A. S. *twcor*, Engl. *queer*.

Da sprengen plötzlich in die Quer
Fünfzig türkische Reiter daher. (*Uhland*.)
Mit einem Blick konnt uns der Feind
Querüber sehen. (*Gleim*.)

88 (140) The word Rappe, black horse, and Rabe, raven, mean originally the same thing, and come both from *rabo* (Late O. H. G.).

(141) Literally: Good advice was dear (*hence difficult to get*), which will clear up the meaning.

89 (142) Zugehen = to pass. Hence, literally: It (that matter, that business) is not passing (going on) with right, straightforward or proper things or means. There is consequently something wrong.

90 (143) **Die Traufe** = the eaves. Compare:
„Wenn des Regens jäher Schlag
Niederrauscht von Trauf und Dach." (*Voss*.)

93 (144) **Schade**—A. S. *sceth*—E. *scath* and *scathe*, damage, injury. Dan. *skade*, Swed. *skada*, Icel. *skadi*. (*Nuttall*.)

94 (145) **Schalk** meant first a man servant, a slave; then a man of mean and low sentiments, ready for any mischief, a trickster. It is in O. H. G. *scalh* and *scalch* (Plur. *schalchâ*), Goth. *skalks*, Old Norse *skâlkr*. Its origin is unknown. The French word *maréchal* is derived from *marahscalc* (an officer in charge of the King's horses), as is *sénéchal* from *siniscalc* (Med. Lat. *seniscalcus*), properly the oldest of the slaves or servants. (*Brachet, Etymological Dictionary*.)

Page		
95	(146)	**Scheiterhaufen,** compound of Scheiter, plur. of Scheit, log, and Haufen, heap, pile.
	(147)	**Schelten** means both scold, and (with a double Accusative), to call one something bad. O. H. G. sceltan. Dutch *schelden,* Dan. *skielde,* Sw. *skälla,* E. *scold.*
96	(148)	**Schildwache** — See note 25. In Modern German we also use die Schildwacht. — „Da steht eine Schildwacht." *Gutzkow.*
	(149)	**Schimmel** — *Sanders* says: The name probably means the shimmering one (das schimmernde Roß) — The great lexicographer *Sanders* is a *German.* — Compare O. H. G. *blancros* (white horse); perhaps it is also akin to O. H. G. *scimbal* = mould; see schimmelig. The A. S. word was *blonca* (the white one). In a Frankfurt document of 1374 we have „ein schemeliges përd." (*Weigand.*)
97	(150)	**Schlecht** — The first signification of the word is perfectly level, smooth, straight, simple, artless; then it got to mean low in price, lacking prominent qualities. It is often used in the sense of simple. Thus *Schiller* in *Kabale und Liebe* has, „Gott weiß, wie ich schlechter (=schlichter) Mann zu diesem Engel gekommen bin and again. „Wären Sie ein schlechter, geringer Bürgersmann." Engl. *slight,* O. H. G *sleht,* Goth. *slaihts.*

Slight has, according to *Webster,* these meanings: not decidedly marked, not forcible, inconsiderable, unimportant, weak; not stout, slender; foolish, silly, weak in intellect.

The meaning *bad* for our schlecht is of comparatively recent date, and so is the English verb *to slight* = to disregard.

| 100 | (151) | **Schweißfuchs** — *Weigand* says: „Der Name, weil die weißliche Farbe schaumartigem Schweiß ähnelt." |

„Nimm das, ehrlicher Graukopf, für den Schweißfuchsen im Stall." Schiller's Räuber, 4. 3., where it follows the weak declension; the strong form is now more common.

| 104 | (152) | **Gründen** = haben einen tiefen Grund. **Gründen** is here used intransitively. Thus *Immermann:* „Daß |

in dieſen Gebieten ſich immer tiefere Tiefen austiefen und unter dem Abgrunde der Abgrund gründet [ein anderer Abgrund iſt]".

105 (153) Compare the *French* for Arabian Nights — *Les mille et une nuits*, the thousand and one nights.

107 (154) **Treiben** has very nearly all the meanings of the English verb *to drive* (we cannot say, in einem Wagen treiben, for to drive in a carriage, fahren being the Verb required then). Its Etymology is, O. H. G. *trîpan, trîban, driban* (Goth. dreiban, Dutch. drijven, A. S. drifan, E. drive.)

108 (155) **Um** O. H. G. *umpi, umbi*; M. H. G. *umbe, umb, um*, A. S. *ymbe, ymb*, Dutch, Dan. and Swed. *om*. According to Grimm's Law akin to ἀμφί, and Sanscr. abhi (=ad, circa, circum).

(156) **Umſtand** = circumstance.
„Was meinſt du mit Umſtänden?
Wie die Sache nun ſteht und liegt und ſich verhält."
(*Goethe.*)

110 (157) **Von** — O. H. G. *fana* and *fona*, M. H. G. *vone* and *von*, Dutch *van*, has no representative in Gothic, Anglo-Saxon, English and Norse. Origin unknown.

112 (158) **Weis machen** — O. H. G. wîs (wîsi) tuon, wîs, wîsi duan = to make known, with the Dative of the person and the Accusative of the thing. M. H. G. *wis machen* = to make one aware of a thing, with the Accusative of the person and the Genitive of the thing. "*Gott hêrre, machent mich ir minne wîs.*" (Minnes. I. 327a). *Weigand.*

The meaning of "*Einen Unwahres für Wahres glauben machen*" is more modern. „Der Trom‍peten kühn Geſchmetter macht mir das Heldentum nicht weis" [täuſcht mich nicht als Heldenklang]. *Oehlenschläger, Grd.*

(159) **Weißer Sonntag** — from the white garments worn on that day by the newly baptized in the Early Church.

114 (160) From wetten, to bet, and rennen, to run.

(161) **Wo** has here, like the Latin *ubi*, and the French *où*, a temporal meaning, and stands for wenn. This is very common in German. „In Tagen, wo der

Frühling schaltet," *Goethe.* „Der Tag ... wo," *Schiller.* „Bis in mein 28tes Jahr, wo," *Gutzkow.*

115 (162) **Zeug**— lit. *implements.* O. H. G. giziuc, M. H. G. ziuc, Dutch tuig, Swed. tyg, Dan töi. Compare Engl. *toy* = Spielzeug. Compare with the first idiom the French *Il y a de l'étoffe chez lui,* he has got some stuff in him. Examples: „Er hat die Anmaßung, als ein Staatsweiser zu sprechen, wozu er nie das Zeug hat" — *Ense.* „Deutschland hatte und hat gar nicht das Zeug zu einer Revolution." *Scherr.* „Solch tolles Zeug darstellen." *Goethe.*

(163) **Zeughaus** = the house for *implements* (of war).

(164) **Zug,** meanings = *draft, draught, tug, train, march, campaign, bias, impulse,* and Plur. *death throes.*

EXAMINATION PAPERS.

M. Henri Bué's suggestion as to how to use his papers for Examination in French Idioms, may fitly be applied here.

The pupil should go over each paper twice, either in writing or vivâ voce. The first time he might be allowed to look at the list, where he will find a sentence similar to the one he has to translate. *E.g.* under Faſſen he will find Ich muß mich zuerſt faſſen; this will help him to translate, Faſſen Sie ſich zuerſt. The second time he should not be allowed any help.

I.

1. First collect your thoughts. 2. I cannot find it in my heart. 3. He had no objection. 4. They were two old bachelors. 5. To tell you the truth, we did not see it. 6. We were in a hurry. 7. May we play? 8. Did she pass? 9. They did not go, nor did I. 10. That girl does not know her multiplication tables.

1. Faſſen. 2. Bringen. 3. Dagegen. 4. Hageſtolz. 5. Eigentlich. 6. Eile. 7. Dürfen. 8. Durchkommen. 9. Auch. 10. Einmaleins.

II.

1. At what time did he leave? 2. We found the room crowded to excess. 3. You will do it, will you not? 4. We have clothes in abundance. 5. He could not come nearer. 6. What is the boy doing there? 7. He is parading his new clothes. 8. Take an orange or two. 9. The old lady had fainted. 10. That dictionary is no good.

1. Wieviel. 2. Voll. 3. Wahr. 4. Überfluß. 5. Treten. 6. Treiben. 7. Parade. 8. Paar. 9. Ohnmacht. 10. Heißen.

III.

1. I am going there this evening. 2. I called with a loud voice, "Come in!" 3. He would not take the trouble to come out. 4. You must not be presumptive. 5. In bad weather we stay at home. 6. She was not in her right senses. 7. He did not mind that. 8. What is *railway* called in German? 9. Sometimes we read, at other times we draw. 10. Time seems to hang heavy on him.

1. Heute. 2. Herein. 3. Heraus. 4. Heraus. 5. Bei. 6. Bei. 7. Hinaus. 8. Auf. 9. Bald. 10. Lang.

IV.

1. The moon was rising. 2. When did you get up this morning? 3. I got up when the sun rose. 4. He said to me, "Advise with your pillow." 5. We saw some charming dissolving views. 6. They always pay in ready money. 7. Are you a judge of old furniture? 8. Why do you mince matters. 9. Trade and industry are flourishing in England. 10. These houses have changed hands.

1. Auf. 2. Auf. 3. Auf. 4. Nacht. 5. Nebel. 6. Klingen. 7. Kenner. 8. Kind. 9. Handel. 10. Hand.

V.

1. Do not pick up a quarrel. 2. What is his thanks? 3. The regiment stood all day long under arms. 4. That is a good likeness of you. 5. Dickens wrote "All the year round." 6. It was all the same to us. 7. He was my father's bosom friend. 8. Do not move, my boys! 9. There is many a good point in him. 10. Now, when everybody wishes to be independent.

1. Händel. 2. Haben. 3. Gewehr. 4. Gleich. 5. Ein. 6. Einerlei. 7. Busen. 8. Rühren. 9. Zug. 10. Wo.

VI.

1. Charles is only a beginner. 2. Cherry-brandy is distilled in the Black Forest. 3. It is not 10 days since I saw him. 4. The tramps were having a scuffle with the police. 5. The crime was committed in broad daylight. 6. She slept till it was broad daylight. 7. Now it is your turn. 8. The woman was not known by that name. 9. You do not mean to say so? 10. Shakespeare was a master-mind.

1. Abc. 2. Kirschwasser. 3. Kein. 4. Herumbalgen (sich). 5. Tag. 6. Hell. 7. Reihe. 8. Name. 9. Klug. 10. Geist.

VII.

1. We bought two black horses. 2. There is an inn in our town which is called the "White Horse." 3. They are trudging it on foot. 4. Ten to one, you will fall. 5. She is now going on for ninety-two. 6. The Germans marched into France. 7. Opinions are free. 8. The river is 90 feet wide. 9. Are your fingers cold? 10. It was in the special edition (*of the paper*).

1. Rappe. 2. Schimmel. 3. Rappe. 4. Gegen. 5. Gehen. 6. Ziehen. 7. Gedanken. 8. Fuß. 9. Frieren. 10. Extra.

VIII.

1. The town lies on a beautiful bay. 2. This hussar sits his horse well. 3. He never sticks to the point. 4. Have you *got* your certificate of birth? 5. If you like we will go out. 6. Yesterday evening there was a halo round the moon. 7. Wolsey was born at Ipswich. 8. Very well, that is enough. 9. He was in a bad plight. 10. That war was very much protracted.

1. Busen. 2. Sattel. 3. Sache. 4. Schein. 5. Lieb. 6. Hof. 7. Licht. 8. Schon. 9. Schlimm. 10. Ziehen.

IX.

1. That old gentleman is dying. 2. She would have nothing to do with the matter. 3. We have several clubs here. 4. My grandfather used to take a nap after dinner. 5. We send for our clothes to Birmingham. 6. They cannot do that. 7. Have you learnt the French pronouns already? 8. That child is looking all roses and lilies. 9. We sent the letter at her request. 10. I should like to know what is your pleasure.

1. Zug. 2. Wollen. 3. Schließen. 4. Schläfchen. 5. Kommen. 6. Können. 7. Fürwort. 8. Blut. 9. Auf. 10. Dienen.

X.

1. They came about Easter. 2. There must be something in the wind. 3. This work is not nearly so good as that. 4. There was a starling with its mate. 5. He was sixty and odd years old when he died. 6. You have been mistaken. 7. I am satisfied, done. 8. He speaks of you on all occasions. 9. The madman committed suicide. 10. How is your aunt's health?

1. Um. 2. Werk. 3. Weit. 4. Weibchen. 5. In. 6. Irren. 7. Gelten. 8. Gelegenheit. 9. Bringen. 10. Befinden.

XI.

1. How many are eighteen times sixteen? 2. Do you know the proverb, "When the cat is away, the mice will play"? 3. To my regret I cannot find the book. 4. He was grossly mistaken. 5. You are the architect of your own fortune. 6. In our neighbourhood there was an extremely hard frost. 7. Who gave you the permission for it? 8. John was a jolly fellow. 9. They had despatched several messengers. 10. Those dogs have lost their scent.

1. Machen. 2. Maus. 3. Leiber. 4. Gewaltig. 5. Glück. 6. Frieren. 7. Dazu. 8. Bruder. 9. Abfertigen. 10. Abkommen.

XII.

1. He imposed upon us. 2. That is a very thrilling novel. 3. Whalebone is used for corsets. 4. The lighters are in that box. 5. It is all the same to him. 6. Go, I say, my boys! 7. May we go for a walk? 8. Three days after, he was killed. 9. You are talking gibberish. 10. The beaten army lost courage.

1. Bär. 2. Ergreifend. 3. Fischbein. 4. Fibibus. 5. Eins. 6. Ei. 7. Dürfen. 8. Darauf. 9. Kauderwelsch. 10. Sinken.

XIII.

1. Well, he said, that is now finished. 2. The headmaster gave the boys a blow-up. 3. William Tell was a dead-shot. 4. The officer rode a light bay horse. 5. What did take place after? 6. There was a draught in our schoolroom. 7. The stove did not draw. 8. The barges left the shore. 9. Shut the shutters! 10. The shops of this town are very fine.

1. So. 2. Text. 3. Schütze. 4. Schweißfuchs. 5. Werben. 6. Ziehen. 7. Zug. 8. Land. 9. Laden. 10. Laden.

XIV.

1. He was a captain of cavalry (*one word*). 2. What are the captains of infantry called in German? 3. A German proverb says, "Many hounds are sure to run a hare aground." 4. The lady was very pleased with it. 5. Did you feel inclined to go out? 6. They fired. 7. I said it did not matter. 8. Whether they do it or not. 9. Not another syllable. 10. She gave him a piece of her mind.

1. Hauptmann. 2. Hauptmann. 3. Hase. 4. Froh. 5. Luft. 6. Los. 7. Machen. 8. Man. 9. Mehr. 10. Meinung.

XV.

1. That is very well, but I cannot believe what he says. 2. These people are poorly off. 3. If he goes after all. 4. He is talking stuff and nonsense. 5. He said, "Advise with your pillow." 6. I drank their health. 7. The boys were making fun of the old man. 8. Do not get so enraged. 9. Not in the least. 10. The expression "But me no buts" is found in Shakespeare.

1. Schon. 2. Schmal. 3. Überhaupt. 4. Zeug. 5. Nacht. 6. Gesundheit. 7. Gespött. 8. Giftig. 9. Durchaus. 10. Aber.

XVI.

1. He is getting on very well. 2. They had an easy life. 3. That was no extraordinary performance. 4. They had provisions in abundance. 5. Those children had no manners. 6. You do not know it, nor do I. 7. The ship is sailing down the river. 8. So you are going to leave Cologne? 9. Give my kind regards to your father. 10. They were inexorable.

1. Gut. 2. Gut. 3. Hexerei. 4. Fülle. 5. Anstand. 6. Auch. 7. Ab. 8. Also. 9. Empfehlen. 10. Erbitten.

XVII.

1. They buried her to-day. 2. Are they keeping St. Monday in Germany? 3. Many Spanish ships were sunk. 4. We did not think much of it. 5. My hair stood on end. 6. Do not turn up your nose at it. 7. The school has a very good name. 8. Never fear, he will come. 9. Does he not like that beer? 10. The interest will be added to the capital.

1. Bringen. 2. Blau. 3. Bohren. 4. Halten. 5. Haar. 6. Rümpfen. 7. Ruf. 8. Schon. 9. Schmecken. 10. Schlagen.

XVIII.

1. How is that? 2. What is the time now? 3. They go out twice a day. 4. They left after dinner. 5. They came nearer. 6. I felt sick. 7. Did he give her a receipt? 8. We agreed to everything. 9. Pray, do not forget what you were going to say. 10. That official was of no use whatever.

1. Wie. 2. Wie. 3. Tag. 4. Tisch. 5. Treten. 6. Übel. 7. Quittung. 8. Recht. 9. Rede. 10. Rab.

XIX.

1. They all lost courage. 2. He said, "Good night!" 3. Those fools got a trashing. 4. This cheese is all mouldy. 5. The town is being battered down from the fire of the guns. 6. The children are upstairs with their governess. 7. He had fainted. 8. I cannot bear small houses. 9. He was hanging heavy upon his mother's hands. 10. That sounded very well.

1. Sinken. 2. Schlafen. 3. Schlag. 4. Schimmelig. 5. Schießen. 6. Oben. 7. Ohnmacht. 8. Leiden. 9. Fallen. 10. Klingen.

XX.

1. All the inhabitants were put to the sword. 2. They were good Latinists. 3. The boys were clapping their hands. 4. A messenger came running in all haste. 5. The waters of the Thames were swollen. 6. That man is so learned that he has become conceited. 7. The waiter asked, "What do you order?" 8. The horseman wore jack boots. 9. Have you got a map of Great Britain in your room? 10. That naughty boy is biting his nails.

1. Klinge. 2. Lateiner. 3. Klopfen. 4. Kommen. 5. Hoch. 6. Gras. 7. Befehlen. 8. Kanonenstiefel. 9. Karte. 10. Kauen.

XXI.

1. The sportsman missed. 2. What is the matter yonder? 3. We are getting new dresses made for ourselves and the children. 4. Cockchafers are hurtful to the trees. 5. The lily of the valley is very lovely and fragrant. 6. Their anger was up. 7. They looked dead and dug up again. 8. In Germany meat breakfast is unusual. 9. A bird in the hand is worth two in the bush. 10. The gun is cocked.

1. Schießen. 2. Los. 3. Machen. 4. Maikäfer. 5. Maiblümchen. 6. Galle. 7. Galgen. 8. Gabelfrühstück. 9. Haben. 10. Hahn.

XXII.

1. She slapped his face. 2. We told her plainly. 3. The winters are not very cold in this country. 4. He shall pay me to the uttermost farthing. 5. My name is Müller. 6. What is your name? 7. There was the difficulty. 8. The regiments made their entry into the town with drums beating and bands playing. 9. He said that was a difficult question. 10. Their very faces show who they are.

1. Maul. 2. Heraus. 3. Hier. 4. Heller. 5. Heißen. 6. Heißen. 7. Hase. 8. Klingen. 9. Rat. 10. Schon.

XXIII.

1. Have these boys already done their exercises? 2. We have newspapers in abundance. 3. I travel to Paris *via* Dieppe. 4. Boys will become men. 5. I want some blotting paper; have you got any? 6. He tried to make me swallow that nonsense. 7. You have not changed your linen. 8. Take notice of that, my friend! 9. They would not join us *(in our meal)*. 10. That has always been done here.

1. Schon. 2. Überfluß. 3. Über. 4. Werben. 5. Welches. 6. Weis. 7. Weiß. 8. Merken. 9. Mit. 10. Je.

XXIV.

1. How do you call that in Russian? 2. That pupil is not of much account. 3. They paid their workmen in ready money. 4. The woman is not in her right wits. 5. We could not help blaming them. 6. They laid their heads together. 7. We are their well-wishers. 8. Do not be afraid; the soldiers are firing with powder only. 9. They are always the losers. 10. Whatever it may be.

1. Heißen. 2. Her. 3. Klingen. 4. Klug. 5. Können. 6. Kopf. 7. Meinen. 8. Schießen. 9. Ziehen. 10. Wollen.

XXV.

1. That girl is not fit for her situation. 2. William the Third marched to London. 3. The Royal Arsenal is at Woolwich. 4. They travelled by the fast train. 5. I smell a rat. 6. He always crosses my path. 7. He maintains that he knows it from good authority. 8. I made the plan of my house. 9. There are many clubs in our town. 10. We were in a bad plight.

1. Zeug. 2. Ziehen. 3. Zeughaus. 4. Zug. 5. Recht. 6. Quere. 7. Quelle. 8. Plan. 9. Schließen. 10. Schlimm.

XXVI.

1. He always wanted to be spokesman. 2. We could not help admiring them. 3. My wife's brother lives in the country. 4. They have changed sides. 5. Be honest and upright. 6. You do not know what has taken place. 7. You will lend me the book, will you not? 8. Twenty years ago I left my home. 9. How long have you been in London? 10. He must have it in writing.

1. Führen. 2. Können. 3. Land. 4. Partei. 5. Schlecht. 6. Setzen. 7. Wahr. 8. Vor. 9. Schon. 10. Schwarz.

XXVII.

1. Those carpets have cost her a lot of money. 2. The governor had officers of forced labour gangs. 3. Take care; I will make you find your legs. 4. He said, "Certainly not!" 5. Do you know the German proverb, "Bear and forbear?" 6. Man proposes, God disposes. 7. The stranger allowed himself to be overreached. 8. Doctor, I am ill; I have no relish for anything. 9. The lion had run a thorn into his foot. 10. There would be a chance for it.

1. Schwer. 2. Frohn. 3. Fuß. 4. Nicht. 5. Leiden. 6. Lenken. 7. Prellen. 8. Schmecken. 9. Treten. 10. Machen.

XXVIII.

1. The money was not sufficient. 2. He is abroad. 3. The old rector has the rheumatism. 4. Are you a judge of music? 5. I might have done it, but I did not care. 6. You are a good-for-nothing sort of fellow. 7. He really exceeds all bounds. 8. I did not know that the poor man was henpecked. 9. The director of that college was pensioned off. 10. They wanted to lay the fault on her.

1. Reichen. 2. Reise. 3. Reißen. 4. Kenner. 5. Können. 6. Los. 7. Maß. 8. Pantoffel. 9. Ruhe. 10. Schuh.

XXIX.

1. Three ships have gone down with crew and cargo. 2. The judge is of tall stature. 3. The Indians were routed. 4. The officer commanded, "Right face!" 5. That brewer will retire from business. 6. England was then making preparations (*for war*). 7. The policemen are going their round. 8. He will surely do that. 9. You ought not to put the cart before the horse. 10. He said he would be one of the party.

1. Mann. 2. Person. 3. Paar. 4. Rechts. 5. Ruhe. 6. Rüsten. 7. Runde. 8. Schon. 9. Pferd. 10. Partie.

XXX.

1. The girls were all attention. 2. This picture will not match with that. 3. We should not have listened to that. 4. We perceived that she was quite exhausted. 5. You are a nice fellow! 6. Over the way stands an old inn. 7. You are not allowed to stand on the paddlebox. 8. She will come back in a year. 9. This tower is taller than that by 80 feet. 10. I am conversant with English.

1. Ohr. 2. Passen. 3. Kommen. 4. Können. 5. Recht. 6. Quer. 7. Radkasten. 8. Über. 9. Um. 10. Daheim.

XXXI.

1. He is very much bent upon it. 2. That will never do. 3. They came and called for me at half-past eleven. 4. She will give her a set-down. 5. That is a fact then? 6. The old farmer sat near his stove. 7. It is about time to lay aside your childish manners. 8. That did not concern her. 9. I was plain with them. 10. He said it would be all the better.

1. Darauf. 2. Daraus. 3. Abholen. 4. Abfertigen. 5. Also. 6. An. 7. An. 8. An. 9. Deutsch. 10. Desto.

XXXII.

1. That would not have answered our purpose. 2. Is Bradford a manufacturing town? 3. That business has a branch-establishment at Brighton. 4. These students are all jolly fellows. 5. This coin will not be current in England. 6. Are you short-sighted? 7. Where there is trade and industry money must abound. 8. The judge was in his office. 9. The inhabitants sided with the emperor. 10. The knives were of different sizes.

1. Dienen. 2. Fabrik. 3. Filiale. 4. Fibel. 5. Gelten. 6. Gesicht. 7. Handel. 8. Kanzlei. 9. Kaiserlich. 10. Größe.

XXXIII.

1. We owe him fifteen shillings. 2. Shake hands with me, and let us be friends! 3. Speak loud, and be short! 4. We shall do it at a venture. 5. Your mother is looking very well. 6. "Similis simili gaudet" is the Latin for "Birds of a feather flock together." 7. You ought to take your ticket. 8. They say that the professor will be called to fill a chair at Göttingen university. 9. It was yet very early when we arrived 10. She is taking to botany.

1. Gut. 2. Hand. 3. Fassen. 4. Glück. 5. Gesund. 6. Gleich. 7. Lösen. 8. Ruf. 9. Tag. 10. Werfen.

XXXIV.

1. We walked on foot to a neighbouring village. 2. If you do not work harder you will never thrive. 3. They were the better for it. 4. She said, "never mind, my poor child." 5. What vexes you? 6. I will not trouble about that. 7. That French grammar is out of print. 8. The English were victorious by sea and by land. 9. Boars have tusks. 10. He walked faster and faster.

1. Fuß. 2. Grün. 3. Gut. 4. Thun. 5. Verdrießen. 6. Grau. 7. Vergreifen. 8. Wasser. 9. Hauer. 10. Immer.

XXXV.

1. That girl is a flirt. 2. We ought to buy something of them. 3. I shall write to you to-morrow at all events. 4. That is quite remote from our purpose. 5. I was shivering in the dark. 6. Nobody knows when the last day will be. 7. We took that servant on trial. 8. We cannot agree with them in that. 9. I dare say he will know that. 10. Service was over, when we arrived at the church.

1. Gefallsüchtig. 2. Lösen. 3. Auf. 4. Fremd. 5. Kalt. 6. Jüngst. 7. Probe. 8. Überein. 9. Wohl. 10. Aus.

XXXVI.

1. That was easily done. 2. They will no longer find the like. 3. I shall do it on my own responsibility. 4. You will find plenty of shells in that neighbourhood. 5. She inquired after your health. 6. They are very popular there. 7. What are oxen, cows, and bulls called in German? 8. Have you seen the horse artillery? 9. It happens occasionally. 10. He stepped in.

1. Bald. 2. Dergleichen. 3. Faust. 4. Gegend. 5. Befinden. 6. Leiden. 7. Rind. 8. Reiten. 9. Ab. 10. Hinein.

XXXVII.

1. Why do you stare there? 2. I said I would forgive them. 3. You must enclose your certificate of vaccination in your letter. 4. That is their look-out. 5. Where is the (*railway*) guard? 6. Is the Sultan an autocrat? 7. He will back out of that affair. 8. My parents went to live at Leipzig. 9. I shall spare no pain. 10. That flood was nothing compared with the one I saw in America.

1. Geben. 2. Schenken. 3. Schein. 4. Sache. 5. Schaffner. 6. Selbst. 7. Ziehen. 8. Ziehen. 9. Verdrießen. 10. Gegen.

XXXVIII.

1. How are you and your family? 2. You never fear, I am here to protect you. 3. We inferred from that letter that you were coming. 4. He might certainly have said that. 5. She never would take care of herself. 6. Those peaches are so fine that my mouth waters. 7. The boys were going too far. 8. Will there be any races run? 9. The yacht sailed down the river. 10. You say then you will not go?

1. Gehen. 2. Ruhig. 3. Schließen. 4. Schon.
5. Schonen. 6. Wasser. 7. Kraus. 8. Wettrennen.
9. Ab. 10. Also.

XXXIX.

1. I am going to meet my mother. 2. The niece does not get along with her aunt. 3. These backbiters have taken away that good woman's character. 4. This day week I shall leave for Germany. 5. I know her, and I can only speak most highly of her. 6. The watchword was, "Emperor and State." 7. Put this silly fear out of your thoughts. 8. My grandfather attained to a good old age. 9. She did not feel comfortable. 10. The patient is dying.

1. Entgegen. 2. Kommen. 3. Ruf. 4. Über. 5. Lieb.
6. Losungswort. 7. Schlagen. 8. Schön. 9. Wohl.
10. Zug.

XL.

1. He is now wealthy, but he may become poor. 2. I will give you what is fair and reasonable. 3. That is a very thoughtful little poem. 4. Our proverb says, "Still waters run deep." 5. He was very jovial at table. 6. This dictionary costs me thirty shillings. 7. Do you know how to keep your counsel? 8. She has misunderstood it. 9. It was right under his nose. 10. Sentries have sentry-boxes.

1. Doch. 2. Recht. 3. Sinnig. 4. Still. 5. Tisch. 6. Kosten. 7. Mund. 8. Nehmen. 9. Nase. 10. Schild.

XLI.

1. It is weakness to comply with the times. 2. The Scotchman had the lease of the estate. 3. That house has been sold privately. 4. Let him do it, if he pleases. 5. He called in a loud voice, "Good luck!" 6. On Christmas eve we expect our brother. 7. Is that the headmaster of the board school? 8. What do you bet, I know what you are thinking? 9. There was a hitch in that affair. 10. You ought to set to work, George.

1. Mantel. 2. Pacht. 3. Hand. 4. Gefällig. 5. Glück. 6. Heilig. 7. Haupt. 8. Gelten. 9. Haken. 10. Gehen.

XLII.

1. This day fortnight our cousin Frederick arrived from America. 2. I regret to say he is not truthful. 3. I did not hesitate. 4. That candidate knew next to nothing. 5. Those were strange phenomena. 6. I will not be dissuaded from it. 7. Even amongst the lower classes such behaviour is offensive. 8. You are a rare bird. 9. It rains here rarely. 10. That is what we call carrying coals to Newcastle.

1. Vor. 2. Leiber. 3. Anstand. 4. Nichts. 5. Natur. 6. Nehmen. 7. Selbst. 8. Selten. 9. Selten. 10. Wasser.

XLIII.

1. I have learned the whole poem by heart. 2. He does not know it by heart. 3. He arrived soon after. 4. Gentlemen, we are disputing about mere trifles. 5. What are you mumbling? 6. We were making extracts. 7. They marched with flying colours. 8. There are many factories in Ipswich. 9. Kindly come over to us. 10. I am coming with all my family.

1. Auswendig. 2. Auswendig. 3. Bald. 4. Bart. 5. Bart. 6. Auszug. 7. Fahne. 8. Fabrik. 9. Gefälligst. 10. Kind.

XLIV.

1. I must take leave of my teacher. 2. Of course, he will never consent to that. 3. I shall do it out of regard for his late brother. 4. My grandmother walks with great difficulty. 5. I have caught the naughty boy in the act. 6. We wish her well. 7. His name has a good ring in my country. 8. We agree to everything. 9. We shall enter into arrangements with them. 10. Agreed! cried the stranger.

1. Nehmen. 2. Natürlich. 3. Rücksicht. 4. Fallen. 5. Betreffen. 6. Gut. 7. Klang. 8. Recht. 9. Überein. 10. Einverstanden.

XLV.

1. The children have been placed in safety. 2. You ought not to be intimidated so easily. 3. The robbers had taken to their heels. 4. Go at it with a will! 5. What is the fare from here to Munich? 6. In stormy weather we shut the shutters. 7. I wonder how he hit on it? 8. What means "Necessity knows no law" in French? 9. Everyone in his turn. 10. The parcel came by to-day's post.

1. Bringen. 2. Bockshorn. 3. Hase. 4. Los. 5. Fahr. 6. Bei. 7. Darauf. 8. Eisen. 9. Heute. 10. Post.

XLVI.

1. They know with whom they have to do. 2. There are excellent fancy articles' shops in our town. 3. The peasantry are fond of common street songs. 4. The fortress held out eight months. 5. What does your uncle think of it. 6. Those little rogues have eaten my plums. 7. I do not know what to think of her. 8. The price was £1,000 down. 9. To put an end to the matter, I said no. 10. There are many booksellers here.

1. Leute. 2. Galanterie. 3. Gassenhauer. 4. Halten. 5. Halten. 6. Los. 7. Daran. 8. Bar. 9. Abkommen. 10. Hierorts.

XLVII.

1. In vain I have been turning it over in my mind. 2. Has your brother-in-law passed his examination. 3. Constance lies on the Lake of Constance. 4. That is not worth while. 5. That is wretched bungling. 6. Have you ever seen a Jew's harp? 7. The King of Saxony will pass the troops in review. 8. Poor fellow, he is mad. 9. The lawyer made the most of his client's youth. 10. He had a very large family.

1. Hin. 2. Durchkommen. 3. Bodensee. 4. Lohnen. 5. Machwerk. 6. Maul. 7. Heer. 8. Geist. 9. Gelten. 10. Familie.

XLVIII.

1. Good day, sir! 2. He has a letter of introduction to the rector. 3. Charles is still young. 4. The soldiers rushed on us with their swords drawn. 5. She is always talking idle rubbish. 6. The station building had caught fire. 7. What is the news? 8. The patient was taking small draughts of wine. 9. It was no go. 10. They removed to Vienna.

1. Empfehlen. 2. Empfehlung. 3. Blut. 4. Blank. 5. Blau. 6. Brand. 7. Bringen. 8. Zug. 9. Ziehen. 10. Ziehen.

XLIX.

1. He often drank too much. 2. That turned out very badly for them. 3. The train escaped a collision within a hair's breadth. 4. The singer (*f.*) created a sensation. 5. He found something splendid. 6. Besides other business this also was taken into consideration. 7. I can go now, if you like. 8. We were prepared for it. 9. They pretend not to be aware of it. 10. Clear out, nasty boys!

1. Übernehmen. 2. Übel. 3. Haar. 4. Furore. 5. Fund. 6. Neben. 7. Recht. 8. Fassen. 9. Dergleichen. 10. Fort.

L.

1. That was out of the question then. 2. That firm has a good character. 3. Why do you not go home now? 4. You applied to the wrong man. 5. Be quiet there! 6. I was meant by that remark. 7. Henry has found his match. 8. That stranger is half seas over. 9. Her heart leaped for joy. 10. There were about two thousand men.

1. Frage. 2. Geruch. 3. Haus. 4. Kommen. 5. Ruhig. 6. Münzen. 7. Recht. 8. Laben. 9. Lachen. 10. Gegen.

LI.

1. She has been sent to prison. 2. We always pay cash. 3. You are welcome to it. 4. The Romans conquered by water and by land. 5. This is a ladies' club. 6. Why do you laugh there? 7. That boy never will keep himself clean. 8. What does that profit us? 9. He was caught in the very act. 10. "Spick and span" is a peculiar expression.

1. Gefängnis. 2. Bar. 3. Gern. 4. Land. 5. Kränzchen. 6. Lachen. 7. Halten. 8. Frommen. 9. Frisch. 10. Funkelnagelneu.

LII.

1. They nearly upset the boat. 2. We have only taken 27 marks to-day. 3. I will sicken that drunkard of his drink. 4. I preferred travelling by fast train. 5. Your life is at stake. 6. What is this thing called in Italian? 7. We never could spare an hour. 8. Was that really so? 9. What do we say in German for "Things take time to be done properly"? 10. I applied for advice to my doctor.

1. Balb. 2. Lösen. 3. Luft. 4. Lieber. 5. Gelten. 6. Auf. 7. Abkommen. 8. Auch. 9. Ding. 10. Erholen.

LIII.

1. Respectable people do not haunt low public houses. 2. Dogs had to be muzzled during the hot months. 3. He is not deaf. 4. You do not know the irregular comparisons quite well. 5. We can go, if you like. 6. When the cat is away, the mice will play. 7. She does not see to it. 8. He let him into the secret. 6. I travel by the 10 o'clock train. 10. Alexander's march to Persia.

1. Herumtreiben (sich). 2. Maul. 3. Hören. 4. Inne. 5. Lieb. 6. Maus. 7. Sehen. 8. Ziehen. 9. Zug. 10. Zug.

LIV.

1. An honest man is as good as his word. 2. Always keep within bounds. 3. What are those country girls doing there? 4. I want trusty friends. 5. Those old men have become quite childish. 6. Honesty is the best policy. 7. You are a regular wag. 8. His three daughters have passed their examination. 9. It is he. 10. It was not I, but they.

1. Mann. 2. Maß. 3. Treiben. 4. Mangeln. 5. Kind. 6. Gerade. 7. Eulenspiegel. 8. Examen. 9. Es. 10. Es.

LV.

1. In the abstract you are quite right. 2. My height is six feet one and a half inches. 3. Do not quit the ranks. 4. "Ask for a favour," said the prince. 5. I shall write to-night. 6. The headmaster used to slap the boys' faces. 7. What has roused her jealousy? 8. How many stops has that organ? 9. I never doubted it. 10. That did neither regard you nor them.

1. An. 2. Fuß. 3. Glied. 4. Gnade. 5. Heute. 6. Maulschellen. 7. Rege. 8. Register. 9. Daran. 10. An.

LVI.

1. Come, let us go home! 2. There was no objection. 3. He is a schoolmaster; so am I. 4. He will get reconciled to it. 5. They do not care. 6. What will become of them? 7. There was no thoroughfare. 8. These singers are not keeping in tune. 9. Those gentlemen are my friends and patrons. 10. Educated people do not speak thus.

1. Auf. 2. Anstand. 3. Auch. 4. Darein. 5. Danach. 6. Werben. 7. Weg. 8. Ton. 9. Gönner. 10. Gebildet.

LVII.

1. As it happens. 2. Shortly after my cousin stepped into the room. 3. It is all up. 4. The business increased more and more. 5. We shall see you one of these days. 6. In our country they smoke a good deal. 7. She said she would never undertake it. 8. He might certainly have written. 9. What did you order, sir? 10. They counted beginning from below.

1. Danach. 2. Danach. 3. Damit. 4. Immer. 5. Tag. 6. Land. 7. Nehmen. 8. Schon. 9. Befehlen. 10. Auf.

LVIII.

1. Have you seen that beautiful view of Edinburgh? 2. Are you sure you gave her the key? 3. That went beyond Mary's reach. 4. That would not serve their purpose. 5. They are coming to blows. 6. Mind his words. 7. I told them to stay where they were. 8. He pretended to know nothing. 9. Well, I will allow him to be right. 10. Have you ever read the Arabian nights.

1. Ansicht. 2. Auch. 3. Begriff. 4. Fort. 5. Kommen. 6. Rede. 7. Sitzen. 8. Stellen. 9. Sollen. 10. Tausend.

LIX.

1. You are very much mistaken. 2. Why here is my sister-in-law. 3. Will you dine with us to-day? 4. Watch her! 5. They were cantering in the meadow. 6. They had not a bit of it left. 7. The ministers were in treaty. 8. Frederick, you ought to go to the post-office. 9. Why, that is a downright falsehood. 10. We wished him a happy New Year.

1. Irren. 2. Ja. 3. Gast. 4. Sehen. 5. Galopp. 6. Gar. 7. Begriffen. 8. Auf. 9. Bar. 10. Glück.

LX.

1. He took an example by their behaviour.
2. That speaker is very popular. 3. All the better for you. 4. These thalers are not current in Belgium. 5. You ought not to speak so rudely to her. 6. Henry is a jolly fellow. 7. Jerusalem was levelled with the ground. 8. He could not remember what he had learnt. 9. It does not signify. 10. If you value your life do not go there.

1. An. 2. Anklang. 3. Desto. 4. Gangbar. 5. Kommen. 6. Fibel. 7. Gleich. 8. Behalten. 9. Bedeuten. 10. Lieb.

LXI.

1. What is the third syllable from the end called in Latin? 2. The doctor cannot utilize his learning. 3. The weather looked like rain. 4. They caught sight of Vesuvius. 5. True, said John. 6. The master rebuked the boy sharply. 7. Those loaves are new. 8. Did you admire the dissolving views? 9. Charles would if he could. 10. She was an optimist.

1. Dritt. 2. Bringen. 3. Anlassen. 4. Ansichtig. 5. Auch. 6. Anlassen. 7. Neu. 8. Nebel. 9. Mögen. 10. Geige.

LXII.

1. You want money for that. 2. Are you in your right senses? 3. They helped themselves. 4. His partner had to keep his bed for a fortnight. 5. Are you pleased with these carriages? 6. That observation passes our comprehension. 7. Why, that is too bad! 8. Mary is now going on for twelve. 9. The battle of Solferino was fought in 1859. 10. He had left everything in the wildest disorder.

1. Gehören. 2. Bei. 3. Bedienen. 4. Bett. 5. Gefallen. 6. Gehen. 7. Auch. 8. Gehen. 9. Liefern. 10. Liegen.

LXIII.

1. They were sent to prison. 2. Come here, my daughters! 3. They have brought much trouble upon themselves. 4. Is time hanging heavy on you? 5. I put that young tradesman in the way. 6. That girl had plenty of spirit. 7. The delegates were received with music and ringing of bells. 8. The bringing up of children is very difficult. 9. That sort of wine is racy. 10. These flourishes are out of place.

1. Gefängnis. 2. Her. 3. Laden. 4. Lang. 5. Hand. 6. Haar. 7. Klang. 8. Kind. 9. Geist. 10. Gehören.

LXIV.

1. You must not try to impose upon us. 2. When will the departure of the garrison take place? 3. Were you at the ball? 4. That is my opinion. 5. He is taking a turn on the platform. 6. He will be here at a quarter past seven. 7. We warrant you. 8. The prisoner was released. 9. Pray, tell me, what fable was it? 10. That serves you right, you naughty child.

1. Bär. 2. Auszug. 3. Auf. 4. Ansicht. 5. Auf. 6. Auf. 7. Dafür. 8. Fuß. 9. Gleich. 10. Gesund.

LXV.

1. Human nature can never stand that. 2. For ever and ever. 3. You must not trouble about such trifles. 4. We have sent for our doctor. 5. He always has got some new-fangled thing. 6. Everyone thinks his own hobby the best. 7. They are not nearly so clever as they think. 8. He will leave this very night. 9. He is out of his mind. 10. They rode at full speed over the heath.

1. Fleisch. 2. Immer. 3. Irren. 4. Holen. 5. Neu. 6. Narr. 7. Nicht. 8. Noch. 9. Sinn. 10. Jagen.

LXVI.

1. Do come, pray. 2. Where are they booked for? 3. That is indeed saying a great deal. 4. We supply these vests at prime cost. 5. You are taking too much trouble. 6. These people stand upon trifles. 7. She has never been in society. 8. That might be. 9. Where did they attend lectures. 10. Professor Reichel is lecturing.

1. Doch. 2. Fahren. 3. Etwas. 4. Fabrik. 5. Machen. 6. Kleinigkeit. 7. Kommen. 8. Können. 9. Kollegium. 10. Kollegium.

LXVII.

1. I will tell you what made me think so. 2. It is quite likely I may have read it somewhere. 3. That man sang falsetto. 4. May they go? 5. He will be refused by her. 6. Those boys will not get on. 7. Does he object to it? 8. I knew the postmaster of that time. 9. The governess is out. 10. They came immediately after.

1. Kommen. 2. Können. 3. Kopfstimme. 4. Können. 5. Korb. 6. Bringen. 7. Dagegen. 8. Damalig. 9. Da. 10. Gleich.

LXVIII.

1. They are always very communicative. 2. The property changed hands. 3. Have you given us clean sheets? 4. My cousin will furnish a substitute. 5. She said to her, "Be quick!" 6. He is taking all the prizes. 7. Do not play the fool! 8. Name a few fresh water fish to me. 9. She is always boasting. 10. The headmaster of that place was my friend.

1. Gesprächig. 2. Hand. 3. Laken. 4. Mann. 5. Machen. 6. Prämie. 7. Possen. 8. Süß. 9. Machen. 10. Dasig.

LXIX.

1. George will be of age next month. 2. Mary is still a minor. 3. We shall in no wise do that. 4. With all his economy he does not get on. 5. What is the meaning of all your shouting? 6. Now-a-days the common people dress extravagantly. 7. You ought to have written home. 8. That is in keeping (*with what I said or thought*). 9. Mozart was a first-class composer. 10. All is not gold that glitters.

1. Voll. 2. Minder. 3. Kein. 4. Bei. 5. Bedeuten. 6. Tag. 7. Sollen. 8. Stimmen. 9. Größe. 10. Gold.

LXX.

1. We were writing to the same place.
2. The parcel weighed two pounds and a half.
3. To-morrow is Good Friday. 4. That old banker is a rum fellow. 5. It struck me. 6. Who would doubt her truthfulness? 7. A German proverb says, "The sun brings everything to light." 8. Those were but vain wishes. 9. What means "Corpus Christi?" 10. That undertaking has come to nothing.

1. Eben. 2. Dritt. 3. Freitag. 4. Eigen. 5. Einfallen. 6. Dürfen. 7. Bringen. 8. Fromm. 9. Frohn. 10. Aus.

LXXI.

1. The workmen came to the minute. 2. We do not see why they have not yet sent the goods. 3. How do you do, Mr. Meyer? 4. Compulsory labour was very common in the middle ages. 5. His cousin is between fifty and sixty. 6. We mean to come to an understanding with her. 7. Do not take my example. 8. The whole school went over to him. 9. He was always cherishing idle dreams. 10. They are pretending not to hear.

1. Auf. 2. Begreifen. 3. Befinden. 4. Frohn. 5. Fünfziger. 6. Rein. 7. Richten. 8. Schlagen. 9. Tragen. 10. Thun.

LXXII.

1. My cousin used to go to London twice a year. 2. They were fondling her overmuch. 3. She sits with her arms folded. 4. The case will not be touched upon to-day. 5. His will was found amongst his papers. 6. I shall not say anything for the present. 7. Can you change this sovereign for me? 8. He was about to go. 9. There is neither rhyme nor reason. 10. They are silly things.

1. Pflegen. 2. Schön. 3. Schoß. 4. Vor. 5. Unter. 6. Vorläufig. 7. Wechseln. 8. Begriff. 9. Fauft. 10. Ding.

LXXIII.

1. Such speeches ought to be forbidden. 2. You were not there? Yes, I was. 3. They turned their linen and their clothes into money. 4. He is safe, I hope. 5. Why, that is very strange! 6. Do you know your multiplication tables? 7. We travelled on an average 200 miles a day. 8. That calculation ought not to be difficult. 9. That was quite a strange coincidence. 10. The workmen presented a petition to the head of the firm.

1. Derartig. 2. Doch. 3. Machen. 4. Doch. 5. Ei. 6. Einmaleins. 7. Durchschnitt. 8. Dürfen. 9. Eigen. 10. Eingabe.

LXXIV.

1. James is between thirty and forty. 2. Do give it me.—No, certainly not. 3. The general has a standing invitation there. 4. His appearance is prepossessing. 5. Boys ought not to be sneaks. 6. Max will not be promoted. 7. Well done, my boy! 8. The Turks took the Russians in flank. 9. You ought not to stand on ceremony. 10. I felt as if I were at home.

1. Dreißiger. 2. Doch. 3. Einladen. 4. Einnehmend. 5. Schleicher. 6. Sitzen. 7. So. 8. Seite. 9. Umstand. 10. Vorkommen.

LXXV.

1. William and Frederick are on good terms with each other. 2. Are you cold, Charles? 3. Yes, there is an extremely hard frost. 4. These people are always living in great style. 5. She could not look into her mother's face. 6. They said they would get photographed in profile. 7. The duke drove in a coach and six. 8. Quickly set to work! 9. Poor fellow, he died! 10. We gave it to her for peace's sake.

1. Fuß. 2. Frieren. 3. Frieren. 4. Fuß. 5. Sehen. 6. Seite. 7. Sechs. 8. Hand. 9. Daran. 10. Halber.

LXXVI.

1. I ought not to have let it slip. 2. How badly he sits his horse! 3. The orphan felt quite alone in the world. 4. Eat what is cooked, and speak what is true. 5. There was nothing in it. 6. It was all up. 7. They are quite right there. 8. Her jacket had a red lining. 9. We had to retrench our expenses. 10. It is just half-past twelve

   1. Hand. 2. Halten. 3. Ganz. 4. Gar. 5. Dahinter. 6. Damit. 7. Ganz. 8. Futter. 9. Einschränken. 10. Eins.

LXXVII.

1. Those boys were down in the black book. 2. Who is keeping the accounts? 3. He was quite pleased to do it. 4. The sportsmen were running across the fields. 5. Is that Colonel Roberts? 6. We have been told by Hedwig. 7. He did not know to whom he was speaking. 8. The castle fell to decay. 9. He said, "There is no other way out of the dilemma." 10. It was not her fault.

   1. Register. 2. Rechnung. 3. Recht. 4. Quer. 5. Oberst. 6. Hören. 7. Haben. 8. Verfall. 9. Fressen. 10. Daran.

LXXVIII.

1. The troops will go foraging. 2. It is a small country town. 3. They sent a petition to the Home Office. 4. He is attending a chemistry lecture. 5. Gipsies are often fortune-tellers. 6. Gambling has ruined him. 7. The regiment was drawn up in rank and file. 8. You have jumped from the frying pan into the fire. 9. Alsace and Lorraine are imperial territories. 10. How is that? said the master.

1. Futter. 2. Flecken. 3. Inner. 4. Hören. 5. Karte. 6. Richten. 7. Reihe. 8. Regen. 9. Reich. 10. So.

LXXIX.

1. It may pass for this time. 2. That observation struck home. 3. Ten and ten are twenty. 4. The prince had lost his throne. 5. There was an end of it. 6. The teacher is laid up with inflammation of the lungs. 7. We hear of him now and then. 8. The general surrendered the fortress without striking a blow. 9. He was very partial to a good dinner. 10. I will tell you what I mean by it.

1. Gut. 2. Fleck. 3. Machen. 4. Leute. 5. Damit. 6. Danieber. 7. Dann. 8. Schlag. 9. Halten. 10. Darunter.

LXXX.

1. Make up your mind. 2. Have they been complaining of it? 3. I shall mention your name when an opportunity offers. 4. The minister will go abroad. 5. Let it cost what it may, I must have the book. 6. Do not trouble your head about it. 7. She found the play too long. 8. Russian exiles go to Siberia. 9. Leave that alone, my girls! 10. Shall I do it this instant?

1. Fassen. 2. Darüber. 3. Gelegenheit. 4. Land. 5. Kosten. 6. Kümmern. 7. Dauern. 8. Land. 9. Lassen. 10. Jetzt.

LXXXI.

1. You will come this afternoon; won't you? 2. How is your sore finger? 3. The sportsmen were riding at full gallop. 4. Pride goes before, and shame follows after. 5. She would not allow it. 6. He made life a burden to her. 7. The pickpocket made off with the stolen watch. 8. Tramps are leading an itinerant life. 9. The boy looks well in his new coat and trousers. 10. The poachers ran away with the stolen game.

1. Ja. 2. Gehen. 3. Galopp. 4. Fall. 5. Gelten. 6. Schwer. 7. Davon. 8. Herumziehen. 9. Machen. 10. Machen.

LXXXII.

1. The Crown-Prince earned golden opinions everywhere. 2. I answer for the man. 3. I did not care. 4. That cannot be, said my father. 5. "Who goes there?" cried the sentinels. 6. Write to him; I do not mind. 7. Do not go on any account. 8. As it happens. 9. That sounded well. 10. They are an unintellectual family

1. Machen. 2. Haften. 3. Daran. 4. Daraus. 5. Da. 6. Immer. 7. Ja. 8. Danach. 9. Hören. 10. Geist.

LXXXIII.

1. His opinion is of no account whatever. 2. We said so; did we not? 3. Delay would not do then. 4. That nasty rheumatism keeps him awake. 5. America was discovered in the reign of Ferdinand and Isabella. 6. So much the better. 7. He has never been abroad. 8. As it happened. 9. We used to go for walks all the year round. 10. The circumstances had escaped her memory.

1. Geltung. 2. Ja. 3. Gelten. 4. Leibig. 5. Unter. 6. Um. 7. Fremde. 8. Danach. 9. Hindurch. 10. Gedächtnis.

LXXXIV.

1. It will be a matter of life and death. 2. I read there, "Admission free." 3. It was too bad. 4. How many times will you get that advertisement inserted? 5. You ought to write down the word in the singular. 6. My uncle had the fifty marks placed to my credit. 7. The judge had not yet given sentence. 8. Have you ever played at blind man's buff? 9. He has fallen dangerously ill. 10. She found it hard to go into service.

1. Gehen. 2. Eintritt. 3. Kuckuck. 4. Einrücken. 5. Einzahl. 6. Gut. 7. Fällen. 8. Kuh. 9. Krank. 10. Schwer.

LXXXV.

1. It was very nice running before the wind. 2. He never knew how to accommodate himself to circumstances. 3. He died this day fortnight. 4. At that time there were no railways as yet. 5. The farmer went to sleep in his chair. 6. Our compliments to your uncle! 7. Our friend has not yet quite recovered from his illness. 8. That was quite correct. 9. If the worst comes to the worst, we shall sell our house and garden. 10. Who is now the head of the empire?

1. Segeln. 2. Decke. 3. Heute. 4. Dazumal. 5. Einschlafen. 6. Empfehlung. 7. Erholen. 8. Richtigkeit. 9. Reißen. 10. Reich.

LXXXVI.

1. They were making a great fuss about it. 2. We deposited 200 pounds sterling in the Old Bank. 3. Did you get the letters registered? 4. There lay three army corps in that province. 5. You must strike the iron whilst it is hot. 6. They are standing six men deep. 7. She will not be advised. 8. The masons are out of work. 9. We had ascertained the matter. 10. She is only fourteen.

1. Reben. 2. Einzahlen. 3. Einschreiben. 4. Liegen. 5. Eisen. 6. Mann. 7. Raten. 8. Feiern. 9. Erfahrung. 10. Erst.

LXXXVII.

1. He made a dive into his travelling bag. 2. The account in question has been properly examined. 3. My cousin (*m.*) returned from abroad last Wednesday. 4. What is the Latin for, "Extremes meet?" 5. Is that you? 6. Is there a steamer running on that small lake? 7. He could not control his passion any longer. 8. She came out well. 9. I should rather wish to go. 10. They are men of sterling merit.

1. Langen. 2. Fraglich. 3. Fremde. 4. Extreme. 5. Es. 6. Fahren. 7. Halten. 8. Machen. 9. Lieber. 10. Gediegen.

LXXXVIII.

1. That redounds to the company's honour. 2. If we were but in London! 3. We shall start on Thursday next at the latest. 4. They were weltering in wealth. 5. That train starts at 2.35. 6. William and Henry were both plucked in the examen. 7. You are too fond of questions. 8. That was quite to the purpose. 9. Our school is at full work. 10. It was your fault, not theirs.

1. Gereichen. 2. Erſt. 3. Längſtens. 4. Geld. 5. Fahren. 6. Examen. 7. Fragſelig. 8. Gemäß. 9. Gang. 10. Liegen.

LXXXIX.

1. If that is all, I can help you. 2. The captives bade defiance to their conquerors. 3. One ought to be on one's guard. 4. We are staying with our cousins. 5. He was holding an important post at court. 6. The quarry is being worked. 7. As for me, I shall not squander my money. 8. They could not comprehend it. 9. It is only 12.15. 10. He is very well off.

1. Liegen. 2. Hohn. 3. Hut. 4. Gaſt. 5. Bekleiden. 6. Betrieb. 7. Betreffen. 8. Begreifen. 9. Erſt. 10. Es.

XC.

1. They are professional men. 2. That rich landowner drove out in a coach and four. 3. Why do you call that Sunday Low Sunday? 4. I have lived in both hemispheres. 5. We shall send you those parcels by post. 6. Cheer up, my poor friend! 7. If you turn to the west, you will see the sea. 8. He said it did not signify. 9. You have thwarted my plans. 10. Mr. Miller is one of the councillers of our town.

1. Fach. 2. Fahren. 3. Weiß. 4. Welt. 5. Mit. 6. Mut. 7. Nach. 8. Nichts. 9. Rechnung. 10. Rat.

XCI.

1. "*Much ado about nothing*" is the title of one of Shakespeare's comedies. 2. You have come at the wrong time; there is only cold meat. 3. What is that to us? 4. Leave that alone, my children! 5. We agreed to that. 6. Austria was waging war with Prussia. 7. That is easily explained. 8. We are boarders there. 9. She had a horror of falsehoods. 10. These are factory men.

1. Lärm. 2. Küche. 3. Kümmern. 4. Lassen. 5. Gefallen. 6. Krieg. 7. Lassen. 8. Kost. 9. Grauen. 10. Fabrik.

XCII.

1. Mr. Hirscher is a professed scholar. 2. I will come at any rate. 3. Albert did that quite unintentionally. 4. Dogs are the enemies of cats. 5. Business is dull. 6. Cheats fish in troubled waters. 7. They are people of sterling value. 8. He does not like to throw away his hard-gotten money. 9. The yacht set sail. 10. This baker supplies us with bread.

1. Fach. 2. Fall. 3. Gedanke. 4. Feind. 5. Flau.
6. Fischen. 7. Schrot. 8. Schwer. 9. Segel. 10. Liefern.

XCIII.

1. By no means! 2. Give me another piece of cake. 3. He won't set the Thames on fire. 4. She was not in high spirits yesterday. 5. The wood was delivered on the premises. 6. We had arranged an excursion by river. 7. She nursed me in my illness. 8. Why, that would be against duty and oath. 9. They were only humbugging. 10. His wife is away from home.

1. Nicht. 2. Noch. 3. Pulver. 4. Laune. 5. Ort.
6. Partie. 7. Pflegen. 8. Pflicht. 9. Stellen. 10. Stroh.

XCIV.

1. That violin is not tuned. 2. They have learnt to speak English. 3. He will meet his match in him. 4. By what train will you start? 5. She felt queer. 6. Why, that is just what I was going to say. 7. The child was within a hair's breadth of being driven over. 8. What makes him think so? 9. They did it at their own risk. 10. Never mind!

1. Geige. 2. Lernen. 3. Meister. 4. Mit. 5. Mut. 6. Mund. 7. Haar. 8. Gedanke. 9. Gefahr. 10. Thun.

XCV.

1. What is the meaning of your sighs and tears? 2. He presented himself at court. 3. She very much envied her neighbour's earrings. 4. He was refused by her. 5. He was reprimanded. 6. "Charity begins at home" is a well-known proverb. 7. You are an American; are you not? 8. Dr. Hill will not lecture to-night. 9. By no means! 10. Nothing of the kind.

1. Sollen. 2. Stellen. 3. Nase. 4. Korb. 5. Nase. 6. Nächste. 7. Nicht. 8. Lesen. 9. Nicht. 10. Nichts.

XCVI.

1. The people are madly fond of that orator. 2. He often shirks school. 3. Many thanks! 4. As far as I could learn that seems to be the truth. 5. He is indemnifying himself. 6. Look at it more closely. 7. He was performing on the flute. 8. Those expressions are now no longer in use. 9. That arrangement did not suit those young ladies nor their friends. 10. The professor was short-sighted.

1. Schwärmen. 2. Schule. 3. Schön. 4. So. 5. Schadlos. 6. Nähe. 7. Hören. 8. Gebräuchlich. 9. Gelegen. 10. Gesicht.

XCVII.

1. They did not deny themselves anything. 2. Club law reigned at that time. 3. Smugglers were numerous on these coasts. 4. Both masters and boys ought to hate sneaks and underhand ways. 5. She will never be asked to dance. 6. In the first place he is conceited. 7. The clergy of this town are numerous. 8. You can send me those books at your own convenience. 9. They are rather hard up. 10. He retaliates.

1. Mangeln. 2. Faust. 3. Schmuggler. 4. Schleicher. 5. Sitzen. 6. Für. 7. Geistlich. 8. Gelegentlich. 9. Gelb. 10. Gleich.

XCVIII.

1. Birds of a feather fly together. 2. His landlord said he would institute legal proceedings against him. 3. Chemistry is his hobby. 4. They were taking counsel together. 5. He promised to write by return. 6. They used to smoke together. 7. Clear the way! 8. He was showing me a sample. 9. That lazy boy has often played truant. 10. Appearances are often deceitful; therefore take care.

1. Gleich. 2. Prozeß. 3. Pferd. 4. Pflegen. 5. Post. 6. Pflegen. 7. Platz. 8. Probe. 9. Schule. 10. Schein.

XCIX.

1. Ridley and Latimer were sent to the stake by Mary, the daughter of Henry VIII. 2. German boys are kept under strict discipline. 3. She has been successful. 4. Can you see your way now? 5. Where did your brother get acquainted with him? 6. Here boilers are manufactured. 7. The news has put the old captain in good humour. 8. Is that German silver? 9. You may live another 20 years. 10. She wondered who had come.

1. Scheiterhaufen. 2. Scharf. 3. Glücken. 4. Klar. 5. Kennen. 6. Kessel. 7. Stimmen. 8. Neu. 9. Noch. 10. Nehmen.

C.

1. Unless they be out. 2. What is the Latin for "Practice makes perfect?" 3. What was it all about? 4. The soldiers picked a quarrel with the civilians. 5. Why, you are playing out of tune. 6. Let us suppose that he will agree with you. 7. Next year Easter happens to be on the tenth of April. 8. She was wearing sham pearls. 9. He wrote to me quite lately. 10. My grandfather arrived a week ago.

1. Müssen. 2. Meister. 3. Handeln. 4. Händel. 5. Falsch. 6. Fall. 7. Fallen. 8. Falsch. 9. Jüngst. 10. Vor.

THE FIRST GERMAN BOOK.

GRAMMAR, CONVERSATION, AND TRANSLATION.

With a List of Useful Words to be committed to memory, and Two Vocabularies. By the Reverend A. L. BECKER. New Edition. Cloth, 196 pages, Price, 1s.

One Hundred Supplementary Exercises. Cloth, 1s.

Key to the two Parts (for Teachers only). Cloth, 2s. 6d.

OPINIONS OF THE PRESS.

"'The First German Book' seems to combine simplicity with clearness, in an admirable degree."—*Daily Chronicle*, October 9, 1880.

"Mr. Becker is good on separable and inseparable prefixes; and we are glad that he gives a long vocabulary of words to be learnt by heart (which, by the way, he prints in English as well as in German characters). The best German scholar we ever knew had laid his foundation by regularly learning sixty or eighty words a day.'—*The Graphic*.

"This neat little volume is strictly confined to teaching the elements of the German Language, and will prove useful alike to pupils in middle-class schools and to the self-student, who will value it as a useful and acceptable pocket companion. The various lessons appear to have been prepared with as much simplicity as possible, the aim of the author being to ensure the success of the learner by easy and agreeable stages."
—*The Exeter and Plymouth Gazette*.

"It is not often that so perfectly satisfactory a first book as this comes in our way. Though it is strictly confined to the essential elements of the language, these are so clearly stated and so admirably arranged that, provided the lessons are, as the author requires, 'thoroughly mastered,' a good practical knowledge may be acquired. The classification of the nouns and verbs is at once theoretically correct and practically easy. The brief chapter explaining the philology of German and English, and that on the interchange of letters in the two languages, will be found interesting and useful. This neat little volume is printed in clear, bold type, and may be had for the moderate price of One Shilling."—*The Athenæum*, October 9, 1880.

From the Reverend C. S. BERE, M.A. (Oxford).

"The book is admirably constructed. It is gradual and simple, and does not overwhelm the young student, at the outset of his study, with the many variations and exceptions with which each step is beset, but most of which need not be learnt till a fair acquaintance with a language has been attained. . . . The sentences for translation in this book are bright, natural, and not too numerous. . . . The short conversations (sometimes varied by the introduction of proverbs and familiar sayings) are also in natural language. They are such as are likely to take place, and not imaginary ones, which no one ever dreamt of using.

"A good *Vocabulary* is added, and the book itself is very handy and easily used. Altogether we do not know a more attractive book for the study of a language, difficult indeed of mastery, but inexhaustible in its treasures."—*The Blundellian*, October 1880.

Ouvrages reçus en Dépôt.
Le Théâtre Français du XIXe Siècle.
Price per Volume, 9d.; in cloth, 1s.

CONTENTS.

(The Editors' Names are placed in Parenthesis.)

1. Hugo, *Hernani* (Gustave Masson).
2. Scribe, *Le Verre d'Eau* (Jules Bué).
3. Delavigne, *Les Enfants d'Edouard* (Francis Tarver).
4. Bouilly, *l'Abbé de l'Epée* (V. Kastner).
5. Mélesville et Duveyrier, *Michel Perrin* (Gustave Masson).
6. Sandeau, *Mademoiselle de la Seiglière* (H. J. V. de Candole).
7. Scribe, *Le Diplomate* (A. Ragon).
8. Dumas, *Les Demoiselles de Saint-Cyr* (Francis Tarver).
9. Lebrun, *Marie Stuart* (H. Lallemand).
10. Labiche et Jolly, *La Grammaire* (G. Petilleau).
11. Girardin (Mme. de), *La Joie fait Peur* (Gérard).
12. Scribe, *Valérie* (A. Roulier).
13. Coppée, *Le Luthier de Crémone* (A. Mariette).
14. Coppée, *Le Trésor* (A. Mariette).
15. De Banville (Th.), *Gringoire* (Henri Bué).
16. Scribe et Legouvé, *Adrienne Lecouvreur* (A. Dupuis).
17. Labiche et Martin, *Voyage de M. Perrichon* (G. Petilleau).
18. Delavigne, *Louis XI.* (Francis Tarver).
19. Moinaux, *Les deux Sourds* (Blouët).
20. Scribe et Legouvé, *Bataille de Dames* (E. Janau).

HACHETTE'S CHEAP SERIES
OF
MODERN FRENCH AUTHORS
FOR
Beginners', Elementary and Intermediate Classes.

The Beginners' Series.

Illustrated French Primary Readers,
with English Notes.
(THE EDITORS' NAMES ARE PLACED IN PARENTHESIS).
Price of each Volume, bound in cloth, 6d.

Aventures de l'Anon Baudinet. (S. BARLET.)
La Famille de Friquet. (A. P. HUGUENET.)
L'Oiseau bleu—La Mouche. (JULIETTE LERICHE.)
Les Deux Brigands. (L. GABORIT.)
Entre Oiseaux. (H. A. DE JOANNIS.)
Le Rêve de Noël. (BROCHER.)
Les Aventures de Trottino. (L. GABORIT.)
Une Vengeance de Jeannot Lapin. (DA COSTA.)
Mon Oncle et Moi. (D. DEVAUX.)
Le Caniche Blanc. (V. SPIERS.)

Bué, Henri. The Elementary Conversational French Reader. Printed in bold clear type, with Conversation, Examination Questions, Notes, and a Complete French-English Vocabulary. 1 vol., small 8vo. 80 pages, limp cloth. Price 6d.

The Elementary Series.

Printed in bold type, with Grammatical and Explanatory Notes, a French-English Vocabulary, and a Table of French Irregular Verbs. Price of each volume, bound in cloth 8d.

Vol. 1. **Bruno, G.** Les deux jeunes Patriotes. (Reprinted by special permission from the Author's 250th edition of "*Le Tour de la France par Deux Enfants.*") Edited by H. ATTWELL, K.O.C.

Vol. 2. **Colet, Mme. L.** Deux Enfants de Charles Ier. Edited by H. TESTARD, B.A., B.D., Officier de l'Instruction Publique, Membre de la Société des Gens de Lettres de France, etc.

Hachette's Elementary Series—(continued).

Vol. 3. **Colet, Mme. L.** Gassendi, le petit Astronome. Edited by C. DA COSTA TALLON.

Vol. 4. —— Mozart ; Pope, le petit Bossu. Edited by F. JULIEN, Officier d'Académie.

Vol. 5. **Lavergne, Mme. J.** Le Vannier de Chèvreloup. Edited by Mme. E. VELTZ.

Vol. 6. **Demoulin, G.** Franklin. Edited by M. G. J. BROCHER, B.-ès-L.

Vol. 7. **Lehugeur, P.** Charles XII. Edited by J. A. PERRET.

Vol. 8. **Albert - Lévy.** James Watt. Edited by L. GABORIT, B.-ès-L.

Vol. 9. **Van den Berg.** Alexandre le Grand. Edited by A. P. HUGUENET, Officier d'Académie.

Vol. 10. —— Napoléon Ier. Edited by A. P. HUGUENET, Officier d'Académie.

Vol. 11. **Vattemare, H.** Vie et Voyages de Christophe Colomb. Edited by E. BIDAUD-VILLE.

Vol. 12. —— Vie et Voyages de David Livingstone. Edited by A. ANTOINE.

Vol. 13. —— Vie et Voyages de James Cook. Edited by H. TESTARD, B.A., B.D., Officier de l'Instruction Publique, Membre de la Société des Gens de Lettres de France, etc.

(OTHER VOLUMES IN PREPARATION.)

	s.	d.
Bué, Henri. New Conversational First French Reader, with Questions and a complete Vocabulary. Cl.	0	10
Janau, E. Elementary French Reader, with Vocabulary. Cloth	0	8
Children's Own French Book. For very Young People, with Vocabulary. Cloth	1	6
Contes de Fées de Mme. le Prince de Beaumont, with Vocabulary. Cloth	1	6
Soulice. Premières Connaissances, with Vocabulary. Cloth	0	8
Esclangon. Petite Anthologie des Enfants. Prose et Poésie. Cloth	1	0

Hachette's Modern French Authors.

The Intermediate Series.
PRICE PER VOLUME, IN NEAT CLOTH BINDING, 10d.

La France Littéraire au XIXe Siècle. Histoires Choisies de nos meilleurs écrivains contemporains. Edited, with Biographical Notices, Explanatory Notes, and French-English Vocabularies, by J. BELFOND, French Master at Westbourne Schools, London, etc., etc.:—

CONTENTS:

VOL. I.
LAMARTINE.—Parmi les Pêcheurs Napolitains.
CRAVEN, Aug.—Éruption du Vésuve.
OHNET, Geo.—Un Cigare cher.
ÉNAULT, Louis.—Un peu de Musique.

VOL. II.
MARMIER, X.—Six années aux Spitzberg.
DUMAS, Alex.—Une Chasse aux Tigres.
BALZAC, H. de.—Le Pirate.
THOUMAS, Général.—Napoléon et ses Soldats.
AIMARD, G.—Épisode de la Guerre Franco-Allemande.

VOL. III.
FEUILLET, Octave.—Le Colonel et le Drapeau.
CLARÉTIE, J.—Bestiola.
SÉGUR, Mme. de,—Les Enfants de l'École.
KARR, A.—Une École de Village autrefois.
AUDEBRAND, Ph.—Histoire d'un Sabot.

VOL. IV.
CHERBULIEZ, V.—Le Somnambule.
LABOULAYE, Ed.—Le Nouveau Salomon.
DAUDET, E.—Promenade de deux Fiancés.
DAUDET, Alph.—La Chambre de Chauffe.

VOL. V.
D'HÉRICAULT, Ch.—Un Épisode de la Terreur.
MICHELET, J.—Prise de la Bastille.
  ,,   La Fuite de Louis XVI. à Varennes
STAËL, Mme. de.—Moscou avant l'Incendie.

VOL. VI.
THIERS, L. A.—Incendie de Moscou.
HUGO, V.—Esmeralda.

(OTHER VOLUMES IN PREPARATION)

The Intermediate Series—*(continued)*.

PRICE OF EACH VOLUME, BOUND IN CLOTH, 10d.

(The Editors' names are placed in parenthesis).

About. La Fille du Chanoine. (BRETTE, MASSON, and TESTARD.)
Chateaubriand. Aventures du dernier Abencerage. (ROULIER.)
Dumas, A. Un Drame de la Mer. (CLAPIN.)
Lamartine. La Bataille de Trafalgar. (CLAPIN.)
Maistre, X. de. Les Prisonniers du Caucase. (J. H. B. SPIERS.
———— ———— Voyage autour de ma Chambre. (BUÉ.)
Musset, A. de. Pierre et Camille. (MASSON and H. TARVER.)
———— ———— Croisilles. (MASSON and H. TARVER.)
———— ———— Histoire d'un Merle Blanc. *(In Preparation.)*
Rousset, C. Alma et Balaclava. *(In Preparation.)*
———— ———— La Bataille d'Inkermann. (L. SERS.)
St. Pierre, B. de. Paul et Virginie. (DUBOURG.)
Toepffer. Histoire de Charles; Histoire de Jules. (BRETTE and MASSON.)

	s.	d.
Guizot, F. Récits Historiques tirés de "L'Histoire de France Racontée à mes petits enfants." Vol. I. (CLAPIN.)	1	6
———— ———— Vol. II. (NAFTEL.)	1	6
Short Stories from Modern French Authors, with Questions and Notes. Edited by JULES BUÉ and a Group of Professors	2	6
Hachette's Second French Reader, with English Notes	1	6
Kastner. Anecdotes Historiques et Littéraires, with Explanatory Notes	2	0

Other suitable volumes for Intermediate and Advanced Pupils, will be found in Hachette's Series of Modern French Authors now comprising some sixty volumes varying in price from 10d. to 3s. 6d. per volume. *(Vide Catalogue.)*

Librairie HACHETTE & Cie

GERMAN WORKS.

Grammars, Exercises, Conversations, and Idioms.

	s.	d.
Becker, The first German Book. Grammar, Conversation and Translation. New Edition Revised. Corrected according to the new official spelling. Cloth	1	0
———— One Hundred Supplementary Exercises. Cloth	1	0
———— Key for the two Parts *(for Teachers only)*. Cloth	2	6

The great and well merited success which Mr. H. Bué's First French Book has met with, has induced the Editor to produce a similar work for the study of German. It contains Grammar, Exercises, Conversation, and Vocabulary. The principal aim has been to render the study of a difficult language as easy as possible, and to make it thus acceptable to beginners.

Bué, Jules. Class Book of Comparative Idioms. German Part by Prof. LENNHEIM and Dr. WEHE. Cloth	2	0
Hugo. German Simplified, being a Simplified System for learning German. Cloth	2	0
Koop, Dictionary of German Idioms with their equivalent English, 1 Vol. Cloth	2	6
Krüger, Conversational German Lessons. Upon an entirely New Method specially adapted for self-instruction. Cloth	1	6
Lange, Graduated Modern Language Courses, based on the analytic method of learning Languages. German courses, 4 Vols. Cloth . . . . each	3	6

    Junior German, 1 Vol.
    Intermediate German, 1 Vol.
    Seniors' German, 1 Vol.
    Graduated German Prose Writing, 1 Vol.

Meissner, The Public School German Grammar. With Exercises for Translation, Composition, and Conversation. New and revised Edition. With 2 complete Vocabularies. Cloth	3	6
———— The Key *(for Teachers only)*. Cloth	3	0
———— **Practical Lessons in German Conversation.** A Companion to all German Grammars, and an indispensable manual for candidates for the Civil and Military Services, and for candidates for the Commercial Certificate of the Oxford and Cambridge Joint Board. Cloth	2	6
Niederberger, Colloquial German Grammar and Composition Book. Cloth	2	6

18, King William Street, Charing Cross.

www.ingramcontent.com/pod-product-compliance
Lightning Source LLC
Chambersburg PA
CBHW021728220426
43662CB00008B/761